The Rose of Persia

The Rose of Persia
Basil Hood and
Arthur Sullivan

MINT EDITIONS

The Rose of Persia was first published in 1899.

This edition published by Mint Editions 2021.

ISBN 9781513281452 | E-ISBN 9781513286471

Published by Mint Editions®

minteditionbooks.com

Publishing Director: Jennifer Newens
Design & Production: Rachel Lopez Metzger
Project Manager: Micaela Clark
Typesetting: Westchester Publishing Services

Dramatis Personae

The Sultan Mahmoud of Persia
Hassan (a philanthropist)
Yussuf (a professional story-teller)
Abdallah (a priest)
The Grand Vizier
The Physician-in-Chief
The Royal Executioner
Soldier of the Guard
The Sultana Zubeydeh (named "Rose-in-Bloom")
The Sultana's favourite slaves:
   "Scent-of-Lilies"
   "Heart's Desire"
   "Honey-of-Life"
   "Dancing Sunbeam" (Hassan's first wife)
   "Blush-of-Morning" (his twenty-fifth wife)
Wives of Hassan:
   "Oasis-in-the-Desert"
   "Moon-Upon-the-Waters"
   "Song-of-Nightingales"
   "Whisper-of-the-West-Wind"

> Chorus (Act I).—Hassan's Wives, Mendicants,
> and Sultan's Guards.
> (Act II).—Royal Slave Girls, Palace Officials,
> and Guards.

> Act I.—Court of Hassan's House.
> Act II.—Audience Hall of the Sultan's Palace.

Act I

SCENE.—*Court of* HASSAN'*s house. Entrance to house on Left. At back and on Right view of streets.*

HASSAN *is seated contemplating the view over the city. He is surrounded by his wives, who are lying on divans. It is a beautiful moonlit night.*

CHORUS OF WIVES.

As we lie in languor lazy,
    Lounging on a low divan,
        Flood of interesting chatter
        Flows behind each dainty fan:
"Is our husband going crazy?
        Neighbours call him Mad Hassan!"
        Not an unimportant matter
    For the wives of any man!
(*addressing* HASSAN) Hassan! Hassan! Hassan!
    Inform us if you can!
        Irresponsible and hazy,
        Unconventional and mazy
        Seem your actions—are you crazy?
    Are you crazy, O Hassan?

HASSAN *turns round on his seat, and faces the audience.*

SONG.—HASSAN.

I'm Abu'l Hassan;
    I'm neither sick nor sad:
A most contented man,
    Though foolish persons think me mad!
The laziest of lives
    I live in peace and plenty,
Surrounded by my wives
        Who number only five-and-twenty!
        You'll find that five-and-twenty
        Are practically plenty,
            If you've a craze

> To make your days
> A dolce far niente!
> Another wife
> Might spoil my life,
> Because you see
> (*'Twixt you and me*),
> She might have tricks
> That would not mix
> With dolce far niente!

CHORUS (*to one another*): Another wife, etc.

HASSAN:
> It may occur to you
> That only twenty-five
> Are singularly few—
> To that, of course, I'm quite alive!
> My wealth is so immense
> Their number I could double;
> I do not fear expense
> So much, you see, as extra trouble!
> I smoke my hubble-bubble,
> And calculate the trouble;
> The trouble I've
> With twenty-five
> Twice twenty-five would double!
> A simple thumb
> And finger sum—
> It's rule of three
> It seems to me;
> Our Arabic
> Arithmetic
> Would prove the trouble double!

CHORUS (*to one another*): A simple thumb, etc.

HASSAN: O Moon-upon-the-Waters!

MOON: I am here, O husband! (*Advances to him*)

HASSAN: O Song-of-Nightingales!

SONG: I am here, O husband! (*Advances to him*)

HASSAN: O Whisper-of-the-West-Wind!

WHISPER: I am here, O husband! (*Advances to him*)

HASSAN: O Blush-of-Morning!

BLUSH-OF-MORNING *enters from house.*

BLUSH: I am here, O husband! (*Advances to him*)

HASSAN (*counting girls*): Twenty-three, twenty-four, twenty-five, O Dancing Sunbeam!

BLUSH: She is not here, O husband!

HASSAN: Not here? Twenty-four, twenty-five—do you mean that Dancing Sunbeam is twenty-six?

BLUSH: She says so, O husband. I say she is forty, if she is an hour.

HASSAN: Twenty-six! Dear me! Who was the last lady I married?

OASIS: I was the last, Oasis-in-the-Desert.

HASSAN: I fear you will have to be divorced, Oasis. I had no idea you made twenty-six. It was careless of me to have married you; but there it is. (*Kindly*) You can have a month's notice.

OASIS: I hear you and obey.

HASSAN: Nice girl. Where is Dancing Sunbeam?

Enter DANCING SUNBEAM.

SUNBEAM: I am here, O husband.

HASSAN: Ah! Is it you, O Dancing Sunbeam, who have told these girls that I am crazy?

SUNBEAM: Even so.

HASSAN: The odds were even so. (*To* DANCING SUNBEAM) Will you tell me what reason you have found for thinking that I have lost mine?

SUNBEAM: O husband, you are indifferent to other people. For when I nag at you by the hour—and I can nag—you take no notice; but sit and smile and babble to yourself that you hear soft music in the air—

BLUSH: How do you manage that if you are not mad?

HASSAN: Hush! That is a secret! Go on.

SUNBEAM: Secondly, O husband—

HASSAN: Don't say "O husband" every time. I shan't forget that I am married.

SUNBEAM: Secondly, O foolish one, you are different from other people. For though you are naturally vulgar and unnaturally rich, you do not try to push your way into the best society.

HASSAN: No. I prefer the worst. I am a rich man, and try to be charitable, but I prefer the society of beggars to the beggars of society.

SUNBEAM: But when I married your money I meant to be in the best society, one day.

HASSAN: We were in it one day. One day was enough for me.
SUNBEAM: The ball was at our feet. I shall never forget that!
HASSAN: The ball was at our house. I shall never forget that! Upper classes? I know 'em, however much they pretend not to know me. They took everything I gave them, and when there was nothing else for them to take, they took me for one of the waiters! No. The friendship of fashionable persons is the one thing you will have to do without—you can have everything else money can buy, except that. I have spoken.

Exit HASSAN.

SUNBEAM: The day I married that man I married an idiot!

Exit DANCING SUNBEAM.

BLUSH: Yes, whatever he is now, on that day he cannot have been quite clear in his mind.

Enter ABDALLAH.

ABDALLAH: Peace be upon this house!
GIRLS: And on you Peace!
ABDALLAH: Where is your eccentric husband?
BLUSH: O Priest, he has just left us.
ABDALLAH: Has he gone out to the streets to gather his crowd of beggars—the tagrag and bobtail of the city—of whom he nightly makes his boon companions?
BLUSH: Not yet. He has but gone into the house to fetch his hat.
ABDALLAH: Go and send him to me.
BLUSH: To hear is to obey.

Exit BLUSH-OF-MORNING.

ABDALLAH: It is unseemly that he should consort each night with tagrag and bobtail—it is more unseemly that his women-folk should be unveiled—it is most unseemly that his contempt for my daily exhortations should be unveiled. He is a doubting follower of the Faith, but Islam hath power of chastisement over her children!

SONG.—ABDALLAH and CHORUS OF WIVES.

When Islam first arose,
   A tower upon a rock,
     Beneath her haughty battlements
     Were ranged around the jealous tents
Of swift-encircling foes!

> Then all her gates did Islam lock,
>> As every Muslim knows;
>>> And through those gates of Right and Wrong
>>> No traitor comes or goes!
>
> For Islam's gates are strong against a friend or foe;
> Her gates of Right and Wrong none passeth to and fro;
> For foes are they without and friends are they within;
> The postern-gate's the Gate of Doubt, that leads to the Camp of Sin!

> Whoever opens wide
>> The postern-gate of Doubt,
>>> Doth prove to Islam's garrison
>>> That in their very midst is one
>> Who loves the other side!
>>> His heart is with his foes without,
>> And Islam, in her pride,
>>> Dost send him from her battlements,
>> The road that traitors ride!
>
> For Islam's gates are strong against a friend or foe;
> Her gates of Right and Wrong none passeth to and fro;

ALL: For foes are they without and friends are they within;
The postern-gate's the Gate of Doubt, that leads to the Camp of Sin!

Exeunt CHORUS. *Enter* HASSAN.

HASSAN: Peace be on you!

ABDALLAH: And on you Peace! I am here to threaten you with chastisement.

HASSAN: Won't you sit down? (*Going to exit*)

ABDALLAH: You are going out? (*Detaining him*)

HASSAN: Yes. But you needn't.

Enter DANCING SUNBEAM.

ABDALLAH: You are going to collect beggars and cripples and worthless characters, and make night hideous with the riff-raff of the town. Therefore you are either mad or bad.

SUNBEAM: Both.

ABDALLAH: I am empowered by my office to say that you are possessed of an evil spirit. And I will recite to you a rhyming recipe for the casting out of devils, written by the most eminent Poet-Priest in Persia—myself.

HASSAN: Don't trouble.

ABDALLAH: It is a pleasure. Listen.

> A man is mad—some spirit bad has probably possessed him;
> And we proceed at once to bleed him—after we have blessed him;
> When he's so weak he cannot speak—our efforts do not falter;
> We tie his hands with leather bands, and hang him on a halter;
> When he almost gives up the ghost, we cut him down and kick him.

HASSAN: What for?

ABDALLAH: To drive out the evil spirits. (*Continuing*)

> And afterwards with knives and swords we lacerate and prick him;
> And then, to make that spirit vile dislike its human domicile, and deem possession not worth while—
> With towels wet we flick him!

HASSAN: Thank you!

SUNBEAM: And you intend to apply that prescription to him?

ABDALLAH: At once. (*To* DANCING SUNBEAM) If you will provide me with a few strong cords, swords, whips, and perhaps a pitchfork, I will give him the first dose without delay.

SUNBEAM: With joy and alacrity.

Exit DANCING SUNBEAM.

HASSAN: A good, kind creature! (*To* ABDALLAH) Will you excuse me if I make my will? (*Drawing parchment and pen from pocket*)

ABDALLAH: It would not be worth the parchment you write it on. You are mad.

HASSAN: Ah! My will would only be valid providing I am perfectly sane?

ABDALLAH: Yes.

HASSAN: The reason I ask is, that I intended making a will absolutely in your favour. Now, you see, if I am mad, such a will would mean nothing; but if it means anything, it means that you inherit my fortune, and that I am perfectly sane. As an expert, which would you say I am—mad or sane?

ABDALLAH: My son, such a deed as you propose would prove conclusively that evil spirits have left you—and I would leave you in possession of as good spirits as my own.

HASSAN: Then that's settled. Go in peace.

ABDALLAH: I will tarry a little until the will is written in case the evil spirits return to you.

HASSAN: Oh, very well. (*Commencing to write*) You are not afraid of my making another will revoking this?

ABDALLAH: No. For the laws of the Medes and the Persians is unalterable, and therefore as a Persian will is a Persian legal document, it cannot be altered.

HASSAN: I never thought of that.

ABDALLAH: I did. (HASSAN *continues to write. Drums heard in the distance*) Hark! The royal drums! The Sultan has returned two days before he was expected.

HASSAN: Oh! I take no interest in court and society.

ABDALLAH: Yet the Sultan takes an interest in you; for the other day I complained to him of you and your evil life.

HASSAN: Oh, did you? Now look here, it is understood between us that when I have signed this, my evil life, as you call it, is nothing to anybody; it is a thing of the past—wiped out, eh?

ABDALLAH: Yes. When you have signed that, you can count your evil life as a thing of the past.

Enter BLUSH-OF-MORNING, *carrying ropes, swords, etc.*

HASSAN: There! (*Handing document*)

BLUSH: Oh, if you please, Dancing Sunbeam says are these what you require for casting out the evil spirit, and she is borrowing a chopper and a garden roller from next door.

HASSAN: We don't require them now, thank you. (*Enter* DANCING SUNBEAM) I'm cured.

SUNBEAM: Cured? How was the cure effected?

HASSAN: By will power.

Exit HASSAN.

BLUSH (*to* ABDALLAH): You must be in possession of a remarkable will.

ABDALLAH: I am. (*Pocketing will*)

SUNBEAM: Hearken, Abdallah! The cure is not complete. Let our husband have this treatment; even if he succumb to it. We understand each other?

ABDALLAH: I think there is a chance of his perishing suddenly in a few hours.

BLUSH: Oh, dear!

SUNBEAM: Tush, girl! If misfortune take him, we shall take his fortune. Our cloud would have a golden lining. I am like Bluebeard's little Fatima. Social position is the one door closed against me; but some day I mean to open it, cost what it may!

Song.—Dancing Sunbeam.

> Oh, Life has put into my hand
>   His Bunch of Keys,
>   And said, "With these
>   Do aught you please!
> But one door only, understand,
>   Is not for thee—
>   Societee!
> The Key of Gold will open wide that door-way;
> But recollect that one way is not your way!"
>   So like a Peri at the gate
>   Of Fashion-land
>   I have to stand—
>   The sport of tantalizing Fate!
>
>   O Golden Key
>   That openest every door-way!
>   How glad my song of life would be
>   Could I make use of thee,
>   O Golden Key!
>   How changed my life and song!

Recitative.

BLUSH: Sunbeam! the Priest keeps saying, sotto voce,
  "You'll soon be widows—five-and-twenty widows!"
  I find his conversation most depressing!
SUNBEAM: Depressing? Nonsense!
ABDALLAH: Five-and-twenty widows!
  Unhappy lot!
SUNBEAM: A lot—but not unhappy!

Trio.—Blush-of-Morning, Dancing Sunbeam, and Abdallah.

ABDALLAH: If a sudden stroke of Fate
  Your Hassan eliminate—
BLUSH: I shall sit and sob and sigh,

"Woe is me, a widow I!"
SUNBEAM: But you'll gradually grow
  Quite accustomed to the blow!
ALL: Time will soften every blow—
  That's a cheerful thing to know!
ABDALLAH: Nature needs (*and gets*) variety!
SUNBEAM: Nature pleads for bright Society!
BLUSH: Widow's weeds may choke Felicity—
ALL: Time and his sickle the weeds may prune!
ABDALLAH: Longest lane will turn to happiness!
SUNBEAM: Why complain of widow's-cappiness?
BLUSH: Steps regain their elasticity—
  Time is a lover of happy tune!
ALL: Time will soften every blow:
  That's a useful thing to know!

DANCE.

Exeunt BLUSH-OF-MORNING *and* DANCING SUNBEAM *to house,* ABDALLAH *to street.*
Enter YUSSUF.
YUSSUF: Hassan! Ho, Hassan! Hassan, I say!
Enter HEART'S DESIRE.
DESIRE: Sir, do not call so loudly! The Royal Guard might hear you and—
YUSSUF: Follow you? They would be more clever than I, for I cannot follow you, in your fear of them. But you and your friends can stay here in safety.
DESIRE: Do you know the Lord of this house?
YUSSUF: By hearsay. Everyone has heard of "Mad Hassan."
DESIRE: Oh, is he a mad gentleman?
YUSSUF: Nay, except that he keeps open house for all and any, and thus his charity begins at home and will end in the workhouse.
DESIRE: I will call my friends. (*Signals with her veil*) Oh, sir, it is kind of you to have interested yourself in a poor party of dancing and singing girls.
YUSSUF: It is in one only that I take an interest, and I shall take it wherever I go!
DESIRE: Sir, I am a perfect stranger to you.

Yussuf: Perfect you are indeed, but why should you be a stranger? Tell me your name, and whence you come and whither you go—(*putting arm round waist*)—and why you were frightened by meeting the Sultan and his guards?

Desire: Do not press me, as you are a gentleman.

Yussuf: But I am not. I am a poor devil of a Professional Tale-Teller, who makes a sorry living out of telling funny stories—and here I think I have found one in real life!

Desire: I do not judge gentlemen by their coats.

Yussuf: Nor do I judge all dancing girls by their petticoats, or I should deem you and your companions as bold as brass—as such girls are—while, look! your three friends are creeping hither one by one, as timid as fawns crossing a glade. You are no professional dancers!

Desire: You mistake, sir! We are indeed all as bold as—as—

Enter Honey-of-Life, *nervously.*

Yussuf: As one another?

Honey: Is it safe to hide here?

Desire: Hush! Why, what is there to be afraid of?

Honey: I like that! You have led us into this, perhaps you will lead us out!

Enter Scent-of-Lilies. *Drums heard.*

Scent: Hark! That is how the drums roll when they execute anybody—just like that.

Desire: Hush! What are you afraid of?

Scent: Of being executed, of course.

Enter Rose-in-Bloom. *She runs to* Heart's Desire *and throws herself into her arms.*

Rose: Oh, Heart's Desire!

Yussuf (*aside*): "Heart's Desire!"

Rose: I trust myself to you!

Desire (*aside*): Be brave, royal mistress; all will be well. (*To* Yussuf) Good night, sir. We will claim this Hassan's hospitality for a little. Leave us—forget us—ask no more questions.

Yussuf: I need ask no questions, for I know your name, Heart's Desire, and I can guess whence you come and whither you go—the Sultan's palace. You are a party of royal slaves.

Rose: A slave—I!

Honey: Did she tell you that?

Scent: How did you guess that?

Desire: Yes; how did you make such a silly guess as that?

Yussuf: Fear not. I do not tell tales out of school. (*Looks earnestly at* Heart's Desire, *who returns the look*)

Desire: I thank you with all my heart.

Yussuf: All thy heart would be a greater gift than I could ever deserve. Yet some day I may ask for it. (*Goes to exit, and then turns before leaving*) Do not fear. The Sultan and his guard will not return to the palace yet awhile. I know their ways. And when they have gone their ways I will return and tell you. Peace be on you!

Exit Yussuf.

Desire: And on you Peace! (*Stands watching him off*)

Scent: He is going to betray us. I am sure of it.

Desire: Oh, no!

Rose (*to* Heart's Desire): Run after him and watch!

Desire: Let me wait here, Rose-in-Bloom. When the coast is clear he will return.

Scent: Look!

Rose: Good gracious! What?

Scent: Your ring! You are wearing your royal signet! That is more than enough to betray us!

Desire: Give it to me. (*Takes ring from* Rose-in-Bloom) There is nothing to fear. He said so. This is an experience. We are seeing life—let us enjoy it while we can.

Scent (*very gloomily*): Yes, while we can. It won't be long, mark my words.

Trio.—Rose-in-Bloom, Scent-of-Lilies, and Heart's Desire.

Desire: If you ask me to advise you,
    Finish what you have begun;
No one here can recognize you—
    We are sure of lots of fun!
        Full of fun
        Risks we'll run—
           Harum-
           Scarum;
       Danger none!
Harum-scarum, Royal lady!
    Harum-scarum, full of fun;
Will the Sultan ever guess it,

    Harum-scarum—danger none!
SCENT: Something yet may advertise you
    As the royal "Rose-in-Bloom";
 If the Sultan should surprise you,
    Ours will be a horrid doom!
     Dreadful doom!
     Dangers loom!
      Bow-string
      (*Slow-string*)
    Watery tomb!
Thus the Sultan may express it,
   "Harem-scare 'em! Watery tomb!"
ROSE: O, 'twixt Prudence and Temptation
    Almost equally I rock!
 Victim I of vacillation
    Like an airy shuttle-cock!
     (*Shuttle-cock*
     That you knock
      Hither—
      Thither—)
    So I rock!
 Harum-scarum, merry maiden!
   Harem-scare 'em, girl of gloom!
 Each of you, I must confess it,
   Influences Rose-in-Bloom!

Repeat ensemble.

ROSE: In danger,
SCENT: Ah! danger,
DESIRE: No danger,
ALL: Illah! Illah! Illah!

Enter HASSAN.

HASSAN: Peace be on you!
GIRLS: And on your Peace!
ROSE: We are a party of poor dancers.
HASSAN: Ah! I am just going to collect a party of poor cripples. Are there only three of you?
DESIRE: There is one more.
ROSE: Here she comes.
HASSAN: The more the merrier!

Enter HONEY-OF-LIFE.

SCENT: She doesn't look particularly merry. I'm sure she has bad news.

HONEY: Oh, I do want my supper! I've had nothing since tea!

HASSAN: Poor girl. (*Goes to house and claps his hands*)

DESIRE (*to* HONEY-OF-LIFE): Have the guards moved?

HONEY: No. And I'm starving.

SCENT: Then we are still cut off from the palace!

Enter BLUSH-OF-MORNING.

HASSAN: You shall have supper—anything you like. (*To* BLUSH-OF-MORNING) Conduct these ladies within.

BLUSH: Ladies! I wager they cannot conduct themselves!

HONEY (*to* SCENT-OF-LILIES): Come along! (*Drums heard*)

SCENT (*shuddering*): I have no appetite.

HONEY: Never mind. I have—enough for two.

Exeunt SCENT-OF-LILIES *and* HONEY-OF-LIFE *with* BLUSH-OF-MORNING.

DESIRE: Sir, I will explain our presence.

HASSAN: Don't trouble! Read what is written above my door!

> Give me enough—for no man needeth more;
> He who hath not enough hath less than I,
> And, like enough, enough he needeth sore;
> But whatsoe'er he need need not pass by—
> Mine is the house of Ever Open Door!

My own composition. Some day I may set it to music. In plain Persian it means Welcome whoever you are. Come often and stay late. Peace be on you! (*to* HEART'S DESIRE)

> "A Book of verses underneath the Bough,
> A Jug of Wine, a Loaf of Bread, and Thou
> Beside me singing in the Wilderness"—

I have spoken.

Exit HASSAN.

ROSE: Cannot we go back to the palace?

DESIRE: When the coast is clear he will tell us—I mean the Story-Teller. Have patience! (*Stands looking off*)

ROSE: But I have no patience! Now I am out in the world I am impatient to be back in the palace. And when I was shut up in the palace I was impatient to get out into the world. Now I longed for the chance. I felt like a girl waiting to see her lover!

DESIRE: So do I!—I mean, so did I!

Exit HEART'S DESIRE.

SONG.—ROSE-IN-BLOOM.

'Neath my lattice through the night
    Comes the west-wind perfume laden:
    As a lover to a maid
      Sighing softly, "Here am I!
Come, and wander where I wander in
          the silence of the stars!"

    In the moonbeams' magic light,
      Cool and silent dewdrops glisten
      Where the roses weep to listen
        To my heart's impatient cry:
"Shall the cage-bird leave her prison, golden
          through her prison bars?"

    Though the bars,
      Thy wing beat,
    To the stars, O sing!
  Let thy soul on wings of music soar beyond thy prison bars!
      Ah!
    O bulbul sing to the stars,
      Ah!
  Let thy soul, etc.

Exit to house.
Enter HASSAN *from street, bringing with him a crowd of ragged beggars, cripples, etc. His wives enter from the house and busy themselves in handing refreshments to the men, under* HASSAN'S *direction.*

CHORUS.

MEN: Tramps and scamps
    And halt and blind,
      Empty beggar and cringing cripple too!
    Maimed and lamed,
      Who've wailed and whined
        Since the morning for food and tipple too!

    Here is truly hospitality!
    Take your seats without formality!
    Drown our care, conviviality!
        While there is sunshine make your hay!
WIVES: Tramps and scamps
    Of every kind—
        Baksheesh beggar and cringing cripple too—
  Maimed and lamed
    And halt and blind
        Take his victuals and drink his tipple too!
    Here's mistaken hospitality!
    Disregard for all formality!
    Crazy unconventionality!
        What will his friends and neighbours say?
HASSAN (*to* BEGGARS): My friends I am a fool!
    'Tis luck for you that I'm no wiser!
ALL: Wiser? Why, sir?
HASSAN: With all impostors such as you
  I am a sympathiser!
ALL: Fie, sir! Fie, sir!
  (*to one another*) He knows we are impostors,
    And he is a sympathiser!
  (*to* HASSAN) But why do you on swindlers
    Cast a sympathising eye, sir?
HASSAN: I've been one too!

        SONG.—HASSAN and CHORUS.

When my father sent me to Ispahan,
  Said he, "My boy, don't dread it:
Here's the usual one-half crown, Hassan,
  You'll get some more, with credit.
A nice new suit and a brush and comb,
  And a tongue that's smooth and witty,
A man may be nothing at all at home—
  But something in the City!"
CHORUS: That's all you want to feel at home
  As something in the City!
HASSAN: So I came to town, where I said that I

  Was the owner of an island,
 Where the sea-birds flocked—and by and bye
   The gulls did flock to my land!
As a sample soil I had mixed some loam
  With gold to make it gritty;
A prophet I'd never been made at home—
  But made one in the City!
CHORUS: A prophet I'd never been made at home, etc,
HASSAN: Now that gold of mine was a mine of gold
  That set the town a-whirling;
So the public and the land I sold
  For half a million sterling!
As the Romans do you must do in Rome
  (Where thieves are called banditti),
But impudent robbery spells at home,
  "Promotion" in the City!
CHORUS: That's what we call it here at home,
  "Promotion" in the City!
Enter YUSSUF *from street.*

RECITATIVE.

YUSSUF: Peace be upon this house!
ALL: And on you Peace!
YUSSUF: A Story-Teller am I
  Of legends and romances,
 Attend and I will try
  To charm you with my fancies!
HASSAN: Lay down your burthen and sup,
  And then take up your burthen;
 Choose for yourself a cup
  Of silver, gold, or earthen!
Exit HASSAN.

SONG.—YUSSUF and CHORUS.

I care not if the cup I hold
  Be one of fair design,
Of crystal, silver, or of gold—

>   If it containeth wine—
>   And humble horn
>   Will I not scorn
>   If it do carry wine.
>   Fill high—
>   Drink dry!
>   The cup doth matter nought, I trow,
>   If only it be deep enow!
>   For, though the cup
>   Be earthen bowl,
>   'Twill hold the juice of grape!
>   Then up, up, up—
>   And judge the soul
>   And not the outward shape!

CHORUS: For though the cup, etc.

YUSSUF: I care not how a man be clad,
>   Or who a man may be,
>   If he be one to make me glad
>   To share his company;
>   Oh, nought I care
>   What he may wear
>   While he's good company!
>   Fill high—
>   Drink dry!
>   For royal wine may sparkle in
>   Your clumsy clay and crystal thin!
>   For, though the cup
>   Be earthen bowl,
>   'Twill hold the juice of grape!
>   Then up, up, up—
>   And judge the soul
>   And not the outward shape!

CHORUS: For though the cup, etc.

Enter HASSAN.

HASSAN: I have just arranged with a party of singing and dancing girls who are in the house to give us a refined entertainment. (*All Cripples applaud with crutches, calling out "Song and Dance!" "Song and Dance!"*) But first, O Story-Teller, will you tell us a tale?

CHORUS: A tale! A tale!

YUSSUF: With joy and alacrity! (*Takes centre of stage*) I'll tell you tales of long ago—old gems of legend lore; or stories, if you bid me so, you never heard before. Terrific tales to make you start and quake with horrid fears; or tender tales to touch your heart, and ask you for your tears.

HASSAN: Dear me! Do you always talk in rhymed verse?

YUSSUF: Frequently.

HASSAN: I do a little that way myself, sometimes.

YUSSUF: It is a usual accomplishment of a professional Story-Teller. (*While he continues his speech, the Men and Girls become worked up by his eloquence*) I've a terrible tale of the "Jinns"—unearthly and gruesome and gory! And the fall of proverbial pins can be heard when I'm telling that story! And people who hear that dreadful tale grow faint with fear and quake and quail and wake in the night from a dreadful dream and turn up the light and—(*All the Girls scream*)

HASSAN: I don't think the ladies would like that story.

YUSSUF: I've love tales of kisses and quarrels—queer mixture of honey and gall—and some of those stories have morals, and others no morals at all—

BLUSH-OF-MORNING *rises and leaves as if shocked.*

HASSAN: Please remember the ladies.

YUSSUF: I have drawing-room tales—you will greet them as fit for your sister or aunt—

HASSAN: That's better!

YUSSUF: I have stories so short you'll repeat them; and others so broad that you can't!

All Girls rise as if to go.

HASSAN: Do you know I really think we'll postpone your story-telling until the girls have gone to bed.

YUSSUF: With joy and good will. (*Girls all sit down again*) Why not summon the dancers at once?

HASSAN: I will. (*Claps his hands*) You don't mind, do you?

Enter HEART'S DESIRE.

YUSSUF: Mind! (*Looks in admiration at* HEART'S DESIRE)

DESIRE: Sir, one of our number will dance for you, by your leave—and then by your leave we will take our own, and bid you farewell.

YUSSUF: Oh, how shall I paint in metaphor quaint or simile daring, the beauty and grace of form and face at which I am staring?

Hassan: My position as host allows me to boast—that feeling's de rigueur—(*Hesitating as if thinking of his rhyme*)
Yussuf: But could language reach any figure of speech to speak of her figure?
Hassan (*rather annoyed*): Precisely. I was about to make that remark. I see you are a thought-reader as well!

Ensemble with Dance and Chorus.
Rose-in-Bloom, Scent-of-Lilies, and Heart's Desire.

    Musical maidens are we
        (*We are three*)
And we deal in melodic frivolity!
        We sing and we dance,
        And we crave for a chance
To afford you a taste of our quality!
        Though damsels of lowly degree
            (*As you see*)
We'll provide you with innocent pleasure—
        We're pretty maids,
        Witty maids,
        Step-dance and ditty maids—
That is our accurate measure!
Rose: To sing my own praises I'm loth,
        But in both
    Song and dance I've experience ample;
        I'll play for you—
        Stay for you—
        Hours on top "A" for you—
    Listen to this for an example!
           Ah!
Scent and Desire: O, listen to this, listen!
Chorus: Musical maidens are they
        (*So they say*)
    And provide us with innocent pleasure!
Honey (*entering*): That our voices are clear as a bell—
         You can tell—
    But of dancing I'll give you a sample;
        I'll trip for you—

    Skip for you—
    Twirl on toe-tip for you—
  Pray look at this for example!
She dances.
HASSAN: Though vowed to the habit of sloth
      By an oath,
  I will give you myself an example
    Of Peri-like,
    Fairy-like,
    Steps light and airy-like—
  Pray look at this for a sample!
He dances with HONEY-OF-LIFE. CHORUS *joins the dance.*

ENSEMBLE.

WIVES.	MEN.
Dance and Song	Allah! Allah! etc.
To joys of life belong!	
Song and Dance	
A life of joy enhance!	
Both are fair	

  Whiche'er you will!
  So go, dull Care,
  So go, dull Care, away!
As the whole stage is filled with dancers, ABDALLAH *enters.*

RECITATIVE.

ABDALLAH: Peace be upon this house!
ALL: And on you Peace!
ABDALLAH: To stop your wild carouse
  I bring police!
Two Police enter.
ALL: He brings police!
ABDALLAH: From Mahmoud, Ruler of the Nation,
  I bring a Royal Proclamation;
  So realize the proverb olden
  That speech is silver, silence golden!

ALL: Speech is silver, silence golden!
ABDALLAH: Then hold your peace—
HASSAN (*aside*): Behold, Police!
ABDALLAH: A golden peace—
HASSAN (*aside*): A golden piece!
He gives a coin to each of Police.
ABDALLAH: And while I read my manuscript, O!
    Attend on Expectation's tip-toe!
HASSAN (*aside*): Now while he reads his manuscript, O!
    Let every one creep out on tip-toe!

        DUET.—ABDALLAH and HASSAN.

ABDALLAH: We have come to invade
    And raid
        Your domicile
If you object, I answer "Pooh!"
    Say that it's cool—
        Poor fool,
            I promise I'll
Make it sufficiently warm for you!
HASSAN: Warm for me?
ABDALLAH: Warm for you!
  I'll make it sufficiently warm for you!
    When I make my report
        At Court
            His Majesty
Wouldn't believe my news was true—
    If a beggar you meet
        In the street,
            He cadges tea,
Dinner and supper, and breakfast too!
HASSAN: Supper—
ABDALLAH: Tea—
HASSAN: Breakfast—
ABDALLAH: Too!
  These cripples you claim
    Are lame
        Of leg, are men

      Who I believe impose on you
          By command of the King
            I'll bring
                Those beggarmen
      Now to the palace for him to view!
HASSAN: Him to see?
ABDALLAH: Him to view—
      I'll bring them all for him to view!
          To prove that I don't
            And won't
                Exaggerate,
      This is the course I now pursue—
          As a type of a guest
            Arrest
                A cadger eight
      Ten, or a dozen, or all the crew!
HASSAN: All there be?
ABDALLAH: All the crew!
BOTH: As a type of a guest
          Arrest
              Six, seven, eight,
      Ten, or a dozen—in fact, the crew!

By this time all the beggars have made their exit unseen by ABDALLAH. *The Wives have disappeared into the house.*

ABDALLAH: Your boon companions have gone?

HASSAN: Why, so they have! How very unbooncompanionable!

Enter ROSE-IN-BLOOM *and Slaves, stealthily, with* YUSSUF, *from House.*

ABDALLAH (*to Police*): Then arrest those girls!

ROSE and SLAVES: Us!

YUSSUF: Her! Over my dead body first!

HASSAN: And over mine second!

ABDALLAH (*to* HASSAN): Do you resist the order of the Sultan?

HASSAN: I don't say that. But I must say, O Priest, after what has passed between us, I consider this intrusion most unwarrantable!

ABDALLAH: Here is your warrant, O Blind One—to bring before the Sultan types of persons whom you entertain! (*To Police*) Arrest the girls.

DESIRE: What for?

ABDALLAH: To be brought before the Sultan in the morning.
ROSE (*aside*): Before the Sultan! We shall lose our heads!
DESIRE (*aside*): Keep your heads now, and I will save them altogether. (*Aloud*) O Priest, listen! You are laying your hands on the Sultana!
ABDALLAH, YUSSUF, and HASSAN: The Sultana!
ROSE (*aside*): Why do you tell them that?
SCENT: A nice way to save us!
HONEY: Now you've done it!
DESIRE: Not quite! (*Aloud*) See—the Royal Signet! I am the Sultana!
YUSSUF: You! (*Looks overwhelmed, then goes up as if dazed*)
ABDALLAH (*glancing at ring*): It is true.
HASSAN (*to* ABDALLAH): I can assure you there is nothing whatever between me and the Sultana.
ABDALLAH: You can assure the Sultan.
HASSAN: I suppose you will tell the Sultan?
ABDALLAH: I think so. (*Stands contemplating*)
HASSAN: I thought so. (*Stands contemplating*)
ROSE (*to* HEART'S DESIRE): Why did you tell him that? That you are me!
DESIRE: Don't you see—the Sultan will think I stole the ring and impersonated you, while you were at home and in bed.
ABDALLAH: I shall tell the Sultan in the morning.
HASSAN (*to* ABDALLAH): I suppose I shall be executed?
ABDALLAH: I think so.
HASSAN: I thought so. It won't make any difference her having come here against my will?
ABDALLAH: Not a bit.
HASSAN: No.
ABDALLAH: Speaking of wills, your will will be executed directly you have been.
Enter DANCING SUNBEAM.
HASSAN: That will make no difference to me.
ABDALLAH: It will to me.
SUNBEAM: What's this I hear? Police? What does it all mean?
HASSAN: The Sultan is going to have me executed. That's all.
SUNBEAM (*aside to* ABDALLAH): You've arranged this?
ABDALLAH: I am going to.
SUNBEAM (*in pretended distress*): And your poor little wives are to be left widows?
HASSAN: Yes. That's all you will be left—a widow.

ABDALLAH: The rest of the property is to be left to me!
SUNBEAM: To you? (*Realizing what he means*) Oh! Is this how you have helped me?
ABDALLAH: The Prophet says, "Providence helps him who helps himself."
SUNBEAM: Don't talk to me of Prophets! (*To* HASSAN) Think of your wives! What will become of them?

> OCTET.—DANCING SUNBEAM, ROSE-IN-BLOOM,
> SCENT-OF-LILIES, HEART'S DESIRE, HONEY-OF-LIFE,
> HASSAN, YUSSUF, and ABDALLAH.

SUNBEAM: The Sultan's Executioner
   The Royal Retributioner,
      Will of course dispose of you
      Without the smallest fuss;
         You'll p'r'aps be led
            To a public place
         By the hair of your head,
           As a mark of disgrace;
        Anyhow, you'll be dead
           In a very short space—
   But what will become of us?
OTHERS: Yes—what will become of them?
HASSAN: No—what will become of me?
ALL: For the Sultan's Executioner
   The Royal Retributioner,
      Will of course know what to do—
      He acts with amazing phlegm!
         You'll p'r'aps be led
            To a public place
         By the hair of your head,
           As a mark of disgrace;
        Anyhow, you'll be dead
           In a very short space—
   But what will become of us/them?
HASSAN: No—what will become of me?
SUNBEAM: When the Royal Life-Long-Limiter
   Has sharpened up his scimitar,

>   You'll very likely ride
>   In a sort of a private 'bus;
>   By a vulgar throng
>   To be roundly hissed;
>   But it won't be for long,
>   So I wouldn't resist;
>   At the sound of a gong
>   You will cease to resist!
>   But what will become of us?

OTHERS: Yes—what will become of them?

HASSAN: No—what will become of me?

ALL: When the Royal Life-Long-Limiter
>   Has sharpened up his scimitar,
>   Misfortune's angry tide
>   Too late you will be to stem;
>   By a vulgar throng
>   To be roundly hissed;
>   But it won't be for long,
>   So I wouldn't resist;
>   At the sound of a gong
>   You will cease to resist!
>   But what will become of us/them?

HASSAN: No—what will become of me?

Exit DANCING SUNBEAM.

ABDALLAH: In the morning I shall tell the Sultan. Peace be on you.

ALL: And on you Peace!

Exit ABDALLAH.

DESIRE (*to* ROSE-IN-BLOOM): I will see if the way be safe—then we will run to the palace. Wait here. (*Exit*)

YUSSUF (*looking after her*): The Sultan's wife!

HASSAN: I have a happy thought.

SCENT: Then be sure it is the only one here. Pass it around in little pieces, a bit for each of us.

HASSAN: I will. It is in this box—in little pieces of sweetmeat.

HONEY: I am partial to Persian sweetmeats. But I don't think even rose-leaves fried in sweet oil with vanilla flavouring would make me forget I may never have another breakfast!

HASSAN: But this will. I am serious.

ROSE: So are we all—very.

HASSAN: This is a drug called "Bhang." Have you heard of it?
GIRLS: No.
YUSSUF: I have; it is worse than opium.
HASSAN: It is better than opium. In times of severe mental worry it gives dreams much more delightful and extravagant.
YUSSUF: A dream—and then comes the awakening. (*Sighs*) Such is life!
HASSAN: In our case there will be no awakening! Such is—! We shall still be dreaming when—!
GIRLS: Don't!
YUSSUF: I never heard of a single man who was happier for eating Bhang.
HASSAN: My dear sir, that's just it. I am not a single man. When you have been married twenty-six times you will see the charm of this drug, believe me. If you eat enough of it you will be able to sit out the most lengthy and complicated choruses of feminine complainings, and imagine you are listening to a promenade concert. I've tried it often. Twice a day. For years.
HONEY: We might taste it.
The drug is passed round—the Girls eat a little.
HASSAN: A drug that will affect your imagination as to make you enjoy a curtain lecture from Dancing Sunbeam will carry you through a paltry execution. I believe a double dose will enable me to imagine that decapitation is rather less trouble than having one's hair cut. I shall reserve a double dose, and you can have the remainder. I shan't want it.
HONEY: It's not bad. Peculiar, but not bad.
SCENT: Things really do seem a little brighter!
ROSE: Yes. Much!
SCENT: Not much. But a little.
YUSSUF: Not to me! (*Sighs deeply*)
HASSAN: What's the matter with you? You are not going to lose your head.
YUSSUF: No. But I have lost my heart—to the Sultan's wife—the Royal Rose-in-Bloom.
ROSE: What impert—oh, by the way, that girl who went out is not the Sultana, you know.
YUSSUF: Not the Sultana? Not the Sultan's wife?
HASSAN: Not—! Why didn't you say so before?

HONEY: I don't see that it makes any difference.
SCENT: Not a bit.
YUSSUF: No difference! If she is not the Sultana I can ask her to be my wife—and perhaps she will—and I needn't commit suicide! That's the difference!
HASSAN: If the Sultana has not been here, there is no reason why I should be executed. That's all. Little enough—but there it is.
YUSSUF *and* HASSAN *shake hands and show every sign of mutual congratulations and delight.*
SCENT: She was not the Sultana—but she is. (*Indicating* ROSE-IN-BLOOM)
ROSE: Yes. I am.
HASSAN: You are? Then you have been here!
ROSE: Yes. All the time. I am still.
HASSAN: I shall have to take a treble dose of Bhang now, instead of a double one. (*Going to exit*) I don't know what the effect will be, but I mean to be off my head before they take my head off.
Exit HASSAN.
YUSSUF: Ha! Ha! This is delightful. Where is Heart's Desire?
Enter HEART'S DESIRE, *agitated.*
DESIRE: I am here! Run into the house—all of you! Hide! Quick!
ALL: What's the matter?
DESIRE: The Sultan himself is coming this way!
ALL: The Sultan!
DESIRE: With the Grand Vizier, Physician-in-Chief, and Executioner.
ALL (*groaning*): Ugh!
DESIRE: All disguised as Dervishes! They are coming here!
YUSSUF: Into the house—quick! I will warn Hassan—if he will listen to me!
Exeunt.
Enter GRAND VIZIER, PHYSICIAN, EXECUTIONER, *and* SULTAN *one by one.*

    QUARTET.—VIZIER, PHYSICIAN, EXECUTIONER, and SULTAN.

VIZIER: I'm the Sultan's vigilant Vizier,
    Who lets the Sultan know the coast is clear,
    When he (*the Sultan*) takes a private stroll;
    Assuming such an assuming role
        As Dervish!

PHYSICIAN: I, the Sultan's Chief Physician, lug
   The Sultan's private chest of dose and drug,
   And follow his (*the Sultan's*) Grand Vizier,
   Who lets the Sultan know the coast is clear,
   When he the Sultan takes a private stroll;
   Assuming such an assuming role
      As Dervish!
EXECUTIONER: I, the Sultan's Executioner,
   Come just behind His Majesty of Persia's
   Chief Physician, who (*the latter*) lugs
   His (*that's the Sultan's*) private chest of drugs,
   And follows his (*the Sultan's*) Grand Vizier,
   Who lets the Sultan know the coast is clear,
   When he (*the Sultan*) takes a private stroll;
   Assuming such an assuming role
      As Dervish!
SULTAN: I'm the Persian Sultan So-and-So,
   Engaged in walking out about incognito,
   With my (*the Sultan's*) Executioner;
   Who walks behind my Majesty of Persia's
   Chief Physician, who (*the latter*) lugs
   My Sultan's chest of my (*the Sultan's*) drugs,
   And follows his—my—(*Sultan's*) Grand Vizier,
   Who lets me (*the Sultan*) know the coast is clear,
   When I (*the Sultan*) take a private stroll;
   Assuming such an assuming role
      As Dervish!
VIZIER: Dancing Dervish!
PHYSICIAN: Holy Dancing Dervish!
EXECUTIONER: Lowly holy Dancing Dervish!
SULTAN: Simple souly lowly holy Dervish!

ENSEMBLE.

PHYSICIAN: Twirling whirling simple souly lowly Holy Dog of a Dancing Dervish!
VIZIER: Simple souly lowly Holy Dog of a Dancing Dervish!
EXECUTIONER: Quaintly curling twirling whirling twirling whirling Dog of a Dancing Dervish!

SULTAN: Tee-to-tummy rummy slummy quaintly curling twirling whirling simple souly lowly Holy Dog of a Dancing Dervish!
ALL: Ah! Ah! Ah!
Joyful gyrate
High-rate my rate
Unromantic, frantic, antic
Tee-to-tummy, rummy, slummy,
Quaintly curling, twirling, whirling,
Lowly Holy Dog of a Dancing Dervish!

As they engage in a Dervish Dance, HASSAN *enters; he appears excited, and from time to time eats Bhang.*

SULTAN: Is this Hassan the eccentric?
VIZIER (*aside*): O King, live for ever! It is.
HASSAN (*regarding the* SULTAN, *etc.*): You are—let me see—four or eight—no four Dogs of Dervishes!
SULTAN: True, O Hassan!
HASSAN (*with an air of condescension*): You don't know what I am. I didn't know myself, till quite lately. I am the one man in all Persia who doesn't care a fig for the Sultan!
SULTAN: What?
HASSAN: Or his Executioner. (*Eating Bhang*)
SULTAN (*aside*): Does he know me?
EXEC.: O King, I don't see how he can!
PHYS.: O Commander of the Faithful! This man is mad from the effects of an overdose of Bhang.
SULTAN: You are sure?
PHYS.: I know the symptoms, O King! He will consider himself a person of more and more importance, until he suddenly falls unconscious. Then he will sleep for ten hours.

Enter YUSSUF.

HASSAN: If the Royal Executioner were to come here and try to execute me, I'd wring his neck!
YUSSUF: Madman!
SULTAN: And why do you care nothing for the Sultan?
HASSAN: Why, dog? Because I am his equal in birth, breeding, education, and personal appearance. I see you are sniggering. (*To* YUSSUF) Will you go away? (*To* SULTAN) What would you say if I were to tell you that I am the Sultan himself, myself.

SULTAN: I should say that you were not quite your own self.
HASSAN: Well, I am not really myself—I am the Sultan! You are sniggering again! If I am not the Sultan, why is Rose-in-Bloom, the Sultana, in my house, eh?
SULTAN: Rose-in-Bloom?
YUSSUF: Fool—what are you saying?
HASSAN: You must be very deaf. I said, if I am not the Sultan, why is the Sultana in my house, eh?
SULTAN: Do not joke of her. It is dangerous!
HASSAN: Joke? (*A short pause—then quickly*) I will fetch her.
YUSSUF: He is mad!—

Exit HASSAN.

SULTAN: Quite!
YUSSUF (*aside*): What can I say to them? (*Aloud*) It is a dancing girl that his mad imagination has dubbed Rose-in-Bloom. He believes himself the Sultan, and this dancer has taken advantage of his madness and called herself the Sultana! And he believes it! Ha! Ha! It was a merry jest of the girl.

Exit YUSSUF.

SULTAN: A sorry jest for the girl to call herself my Rose-in-Bloom—to bring contempt upon the Queen! She shall be punished. And this Hassan too shall be cured of Bhang-eating. (*To* VIZIER, *etc.*) Go, all of you, change your disguise for your official dress, and return hither at once with the Royal Guards. Accept this madman's story—treat him as if he were the Sultan—confirm his statement that Hassan and the Sultan are the same—and conduct him to the palace, willy-nilly. Leave me here, and leave the punishment of this impudent dancer to me. Go, and return quickly.
ALL: We hear you and obey.

Exeunt VIZIER, PHYSICIAN, *and* EXECUTIONER.

FINALE OF ACT I.

Girls enter from house.
GIRLS: Oh, luckless hour!
    Oh, dreadful day!
  Oh, quake and cower!
    Oh, grief display!
Let tears be shed!

    Oh, weep and wail:
  Throw dust on head,
      And rend each veil!
SUNBEAM (*entering*): Oh, beat the breast!
     Oh, slap the face!
  Grief so expressed
    Is full of grace!
With BLUSH-OF-MORNING, *who has entered, and others.*
  Oh, luckless hour!
    Oh, dreadful day!
SULTAN: Oh, ladies what assails you?
SUNBEAM: 'Tis our husband!
  He has gone mad! Our luckless husband Hassan!
SULTAN: Nay, nay!
SUNBEAM: Yea, yea! He swears he is the Sultan!
SULTAN: Dost thou forget the saying of the Prophet—
  "Sound sense has often senseless sound,"
  And "Truth than fiction stranger may be found"?
SUNBEAM: What mean you?
SULTAN: That, perchance, he is the Sultan!
SUNBEAM: Our husband is the Sultan! How?
SULTAN: Oh, listen!
  You'll understand that now and then,
  Eccentric and peculiar men,
  Though undetected by their wives,
  Have led respected double lives!
SUNBEAM and BLUSH: We've heard of men who, now and then,
  Have led disgraceful double lives!
SULTAN: Throughout the day (when you would guess
  He was away at business)
  His palace he perhaps has sought!
  His nature deeper than you thought!
SUNBEAM and BLUSH: His business he mentioned less
  Than quite an honest husband ought!
SUNBEAM, BLUSH, and SULTAN: Alas that men
  Should now and then
  Lead unsuspected double lives!
Drums heard in the distance.
SUNBEAM and BLUSH: Hark the distant roll of drums!

SULTAN: Nearer—nearer—nearer!
SUNBEAM and BLUSH: 'Tis the Sultan's guard that comes!
SULTAN: Nothing could be clearer!
SUNBEAM and BLUSH: Marching quickly down the street,
　　Faster, faster, faster!
SULTAN: Doubtless they have come to meet
　　Hassan—their Royal Master!
ALL: Hark the distant roll of drums! etc.

The SULTAN's *Guards enter.*

GUARDS: With martial gate—
　　With kettle-drums—
　　(*Metal drums*)
　　　　All complete—
　　We've marched in state—
　　　　While boys silly
　　　　Noisily
　　　　　　Dogged our feet!
　　Gallant company
　　Sworn to thump any
　　Lack of loyalty
　　　　In the street!
　　Guards of Royalty!
　　Keen to kill any
　　Dogs of villainy
　　　　In the street!
　　Kettle-drums (*metal drums*)
　　Rattle tunes (*battle tunes*)—
　　Boys silly noisily
　　Halloaing following,
　　　　Down the street!

Enter the GRAND VIZIER, PHYSICIAN-IN-CHIEF, *and* ROYAL EXECUTIONER, *in their official dresses.*

TRIO: Attended by these Palace Warders,
　　　　Each of us now arrives—
　　　　　　The Grand Vizier—
　　　　　　　　Physician-in-Chief—
　　　　　　　　　　And Royal Executioner!
　　Obedient to the Sultan's orders,
　　　　Carrying to his wives

   Some news, we fear,
    Beyond their belief—
     Attend to what we now aver!
CHORUS: Some news, they fear, etc.
VIZIER: He whom you call Hassan—
   (*Prepare for great surprise*)—
 Is quite another man—
  The Sultan in disguise!
SUNBEAM: Our husband, our Hassan—
BLUSH: The Sultan in disguise!
CHORUS: The Sultan in disguise!
PHYSICIAN: Endeavour, if you can,
  This fact to realise;
 The Sultan is Hassan,
  And vice-versa-wise!
SUNBEAM: The Sultan is Hassan,
BLUSH: And vice-versa-wise!
CHORUS: The Sultan is Hassan, etc.
EXECUTIONER: Each is another man—
  That is, id est, or viz,
 The Sultan is Hassan,
  Hassan the Sultan is!
SUNBEAM: The Sultan is Hassan!
BLUSH: Hassan the Sultan is!
CHORUS: The Sultan is Hassan, etc.
SULTAN: Distinguish, if you can,
  Their mixed identities:
 The Sultan is Hassan!
  Hassan the Sultan is!
SUNBEAM: The Sultan is Hassan!
BLUSH: Hassan the Sultan is!
ALL: The Sultan is Hassan, etc.
SUNBEAM: See, here he comes! Oh, recollect
  To grovel on the floor!
 Nor high-flown compliments neglect,
  Wrapped up in metaphor!
WOMEN: Oh, fit the arrows of respect
  To bows of metaphor,
 And flights of flattery direct

   At him whom we adore!
  To load the camel of good taste
   With bales of welcome haste!
  Invite the Sultan to the tent
   Of Eastern compliment!
ALL: Let Adulation's pleasant breeze
   His Royal nostrils reach,
  Perfumed with spice of similes
   And fragrant flowers of speech!
  Let dull and leaden-coloured clouds
   Of ordinary crowds
  Before the Sun of Royal Pride
   Respectfully divide!

HASSAN *enters, leading* ROSE-IN-BLOOM, *who is veiled; as she passes the* SULTAN, *she draws her veil closer.* HASSAN *is met by the* EXECUTIONER, *who introduces himself to him, making obeisance.*

HASSAN: I am the Sultan, and I now
   Shall introduce to you
  The fair Sultana, and allow
   Her face to be one view!
SUNBEAM: Oh, husband dear!
HASSAN: Avaunt, avaunt!
   Oh, woman gray and gaunt!
BLUSH: She is Sultana!
HASSAN: Go away!
   Oh, woman gaunt and gray!
  (*to* ROSE) Veiled so thickly,
   Royal lady,
    How can I your presence prove?
  Therefore quickly,
   O Zubeydeh,
    If you please that veil remove!

      ENSEMBLE.

WIVES.	SULTAN and MEN.
Fate is prickly!	Thinking thickly
In the heyday	Singer shady
Of success he doth remove	My/His Sultana will he prove!

      Favours quickly   Truly quickly
      To a shady   Make a lady,
        Girl of lowest social groove! Mate for King in single move!
ROSE: Hassan! Thy pity I entreat
    And at thy feet
        A suppliant, lo! I kneel;
  Respect my maiden modesty
      I beg of thee—
        Turn not from my appeal!
Thine oriental etiquette
    Dost thou forget?
To force a maid to raise her veil
    Before a male?
CHORUS: Turn not, turn not, Hassan!

SCENT-OF-LILIES, HEART'S DESIRE, *and* HONEY-OF-LIFE *enter veiled with* YUSSUF.

HASSAN (*to* ROSE): O lady, do not fail
    Your life or death to choose!
  Remove your modest veil
    At once, or—
ROSE (*in desperation*): I refuse!
HASSAN: Then, Executioner,
    With scimitar await;
  Perhaps you'll kindly her
    At once decapitate!
ALL: Oh, horror!
ROYAL SLAVES: Mistress!
YUSSUF: I will speak!
ROSE: Nay, nay! 'Tis Fate—it has been written!
EXECUTIONER (*to* SULTAN): Shall I slay her?
SULTAN: Yes; obey in all things.
EXECUTIONER: I obey!
HASSAN: The signal take from me!
    It will be very brief:
  I'll say, "One, two, three,"
    Then drop my handkerchief!
ALL: Just "one" and "two" and "three,"
    Then drop his handkerchief!
HASSAN: One!

ROYAL SLAVES: Can naught be done?
HASSAN: Two!
ROSE: What can ye do?
HASSAN *begins to stagger, and is unable to speak.*
ALL (*watching* HASSAN): Like a leaf
    He shakes with palsy!
  Handkerchief
    Will never fall—see!
  He himself will fall instead! (*He falls*)
  He has fallen—fallen dead!
ROSE: Oh, sweet reprieve!
ROYAL SLAVES: Oh, loudly grieve!
  Hassan is dead!
CHORUS: The Sultan dead!
MEN: The Sultan dead! (*Laughing*)
SULTAN, 3 MEN: Ho, ho, ho, ho!
  The Sultan's dead!
PHYSICIAN: Not so! He will be better soon!
  (*Aside to* SULTAN) It is the drug! (*Aloud*) It is a swoon!
WIVES: It is a swoon! O joy! O joy!
SULTAN: Conduct him to the palace!
HASSAN *is put into the Royal litter.*

ENSEMBLE.

MEN: With martial gait,
    With kettle-drums
    (*Metal-drums*)
      All complete!
  Gallant company
  Sworn to thump any
  Lack of loyalty
    In the street—
  Kettle-drums (*metal drums*)
  Rattle tunes (*battle tunes*)
  Halloaing down the street.

WIVES.	ROSE, SLAVES.
Suicidal	Homicidal

Was our sadness;	Was his madness!
Fortune tidal	Fortune tidal
Turns to gladness!	Turns to gladness!
We are Royal Ladies now!	Safe the Royal ladies now!

ALL: Conduct him to the palace, and
    To mark well mark his coming,
  Commence, O loyal Royal band,
    Your (*metal*) kettle drumming!

HASSAN *is placed in the Royal litter; the Guards prepare to conduct him forth.*

END OF ACT I

Act II

Scene.—*Open audience hall in the* Sultan's *palace.* Heart's Desire *discovered.*

Duet.—Heart's Desire and Yussuf.

Desire: Oh, what is love?
    A song from heart to heart;
      When each doth compliment
    Its counterpart.
Oh, where is love?
    'Tis ever near at hand;
      Where earth and heaven meet
    In fairyland.
Oh, why is love?
    It maketh us to see
      That Heaven may be reached
By you or me;
By bond or free!

Yussuf *enters.*
    The Song of self
      Is but a melody;
Yussuf: Love lends of sympathy
    A counter-theme;
Both: And life becomes a dream
    Of Heaven's harmony.

Yussuf: Heart's Desire!

Desire: There! I thought I heard your voice. How did you pass the gates? And where have you come from? And why are you so ragged?

Yussuf: I have not passed the gates, for I passed the night in a rose bush in the Royal garden.

Desire: But why?

Yussuf: When I had seen you enter the Palace last night, out of breath, but in the nick of time—I did not leave the garden!

Desire: Oh, that was foolish!

Yussuf: I forgot I was in the garden, when you left it; for you took the perfume and the moonlight with you.

Enter HONEY-OF-LIFE *and* SCENT-OF-LILIES.

DESIRE: And I thought I had left Fairyland outside—with you.

HONEY: Breakfast is ready!

SCENT (*to* YUSSUF): What are you doing here?

YUSSUF: I am waiting to see the Sultan, when he gives public audience, to ask him to give me my Heart's Desire; to tell him frankly and openly and proudly how and when I met her, that I love her, and want her for my wife.

HONEY: I wouldn't do that.

SCENT: No, I don't think that would be wise.

DESIRE: Why not, pray?

HONEY: Oh, we're not jealous—don't think that.

SCENT: Some people notice us, you know.

HONEY: The Grand Vizier is quite good enough for me!

SCENT: The Royal Executioner is all I want!

HONEY: But if you blurt out how and when you met us we shall be thrown down a well. We've found that out.

SCENT: I have been sitting on the Executioner's knee, looking at his illustrated Book of Tortures. That's what happens to girls who disguise themselves and leave the Harem. A deep—

HONEY: Dark—

DESIRE: Dry—

YUSSUF: Well!

DESIRE (*to* YUSSUF): Perhaps it would be wise to disguise the facts, dear, a little, if you can—to the Sultan.

YUSSUF: I am a Story-Teller by profession—not in private life. Can you marry me if I tell deliberate falsehoods?

DESIRE: Well, darling, I sha'n't be able to if you don't—that's the point.

SCENT: That's it.

HONEY: In a nutshell.

QUARTET.—SCENT-OF-LILIES, HEART'S DESIRE,
HONEY-OF-LIFE, *and* YUSSUF.

GIRLS: If you or I should tell the truth
    We all shall be executed,
  So won't you try, O noble-minded youth,
    To tell the truth diluted?
As we all shall be thrown down a well,

   Pell-mell,
   If the truth we tell,
   (*You and I as well*),
  In a heap down a deep dark well—
YUSSUF: Well, well!
   We'll tell the truth diluted!
ALL (*to one another*):
  As I'm loth that we both
  Take a leap in a heap,
  Down a steep and a deep, dark well,
    Well, well?
   We'll tell the truth diluted!
   Just a little tarradiddle-iddle-id diluted!
YUSSUF: As you and I, the truth to tell,
   Have naught but the truth to dread, dear,
  We'll let Truth lie at the bottom of a well—
   Or we shall be there instead, dear!
  As we both shall be cast down a well,
    Pell-mell,
    If the truth we tell,
    (*You and I as well*),
  Very fast down a nasty well—
GIRLS: Well, well!
   We'll tell a fib instead, dear!
ALL (*to one another*):
  As I'm loth that we both
  At the last shall be cast
  Very fast down a nasty well,
    Well, well,
   We'll tell a fib instead, dear!
  Just a little tarradiddle idyll fib instead, dear!
DANCE *and Exeunt.*
The Court Slaves and Officials enter, Men and Girls.

      CHORUS.

From Morning Prayer
  The Sultan of Persia comes!
Let trumpets blare

    And loudly attack the drums!
  The flutes as well
    Including the quaint bassoon,
  And let them boldly blow
  An apropos
    And popular Persian tune!
  Your bodies bend!
    Your popular Sultan comes!
  Your hands extend!
    Respectfully cross your thumbs!
  And with salaam
    Endeavour to sing (*or croon*)
  In key that's quite correct
  (*As he'll expect*)
    A popular Persian tune!

VIZIER (*entering*): Outside a mob
    Of people expectant hums;
  Their pulses throb—
    Their popular Sultan comes!
  And when they see
    Their popular Sultan soon
  They'll all break out
  And sing (*or shout*)
    This popular Persian tune!

PHYSICIAN and EXECUTIONER (*entering*):
  Good new we bring—
    Your popular Sultan comes!
  Upon him fling
    Selected encomiums!
  Address him as
    The Sun or the Rising Moon;
  And don't forget
  Your praise to set
    To a popular Persian tune!

CHORUS: From Morning Prayer, etc.

The SULTAN *enters. Everyone is prostrated.*

SULTAN: Are the Royal Slave Girls and Officials all present?

VIZIER: Yes, O King!

SULTAN: Where is the man Hassan?

VIZIER: O King, he is still sleeping from the effect of Bhang.
SULTAN: Last night he boasted he was as good as I!
VIZIER: Shall he die, O King?
PHYS.: For the lie, O King?
EXEC.: Shall I, O King? (*Drawing scimitar*)
SULTAN: No, no.
ALL: We hear you and obey.
SULTAN: When he said he was as good as I he may have spoken the truth. He is the first man who has ever said such a thing—to my face; and he has given me an idea. Take him, while he still sleeps, and dress him in a royal robe, and put a crown upon his head—(*Taking off his own crown*)—and when he wakes, see that he finds himself seated on the throne.
VIZIER: The throne, O King?
PHYS.: Your own, O King?
SULTAN: Yes.
ALL: We hear you and obey.
SULTAN: And see that he is treated exactly as if he were Sultan—in every respect. See that you treat me exactly as if I were not Sultan—with no respect. You can begin at once by assuming a perpendicular position.
ALL: We hear you and obey.
VIZIER (*kneeling*): O King, it will be impossible to treat another as we should treat you!
SULTAN: Oh, no, not at all. If I find the experiment successful, I shall leave him here to be grovelled to, while I go for a few weeks to the seaside, disguised as a cheap tripper. The truth is—I don't want to offend you—but I'm a little tired of you all—just a leetle bit tired of seeing everybody crawling about on their stomachs. (*Lifting up* VIZIER) I don't blame you. I know you can't help it. I know you're unhappy now, because you're not cringing, aren't you? Well, well, I won't be cruel—down you get.
VIZIER (*kneeling*): O King, this is not a natural attitude. But it is natural to be unnatural when Kings are about.
SULTAN: Exactly. It's human nature. Bless you, there's nothing new in that. People talk about Society nowadays being artificial. Not a bit. Modern manners are only original human nature some years in bottle.

Song.—Sultan and Chorus.

    Let a satirist enumerate a catalogue of crimes
    Though he label them the outcome of our shallow modern times;
    Yet a Persian Punch's pencil, in a prehistoric peep,
    Would show us human nature just as shallow—or as deep.
    It is money more than manners nowadays that make a man;
    And a man may make his money in such manner as he can;
    And the more he makes of it, the more his friends will make of him—
    That has always been the way since human sharks began to swim!
        And cynics may complain
           That Society is mixed;
        But I gather in the main
           Its ingredients are fixed;
    And Society has always been a sort of "ginger-pop,"
    The dregs are at the bottom, and the froth is at the top!
Chorus: And Society has always been, etc.
Sultan: Now philosophy may frown upon the follies of the froth—
    Where bounce has beaten brains and vulgar shoddy's counted cloth,
    Where sentiment is "silly," and politeness "out of date,"
    And hearts, instead of golden, are a cheap electro-plate;
    But a woman is a woman, and a man is but a man,
    And the froth has always floated ever since the world began;
    And the froth of human nature is the feeble-minded mob
    Of animated fashion-plates that make the genus "snob."
        And cynics may complain
           That Society is mixed;
        I am ready to maintain
           Its ingredients are fixed;
    And the world of men and women is a social "ginger-pop,"
    The dregs are at the bottom, and the froth is at the top!
Chorus: And the world of men and women, etc.
Exeunt Chorus (*and* Executioner)
Sultan (*to* Vizier, *who has again prostrated himself*): Dear, dear! Please stand up! I do think that even a Sultan's Court officials might occasionally be upright.
Vizier (*rising*): O King, the light of your countenance blinds me!
Sultan: Well, I'll turn my face away for a little, and you can get used to the notion comfortably. Understand, I want you to treat me as

nobody of any consequence—quite your own equal. Keep repeating that to yourself—you'll soon grow accustomed to the idea. (*Turns his back*)

VIZIER: O King, the idea is painful to me!

SULTAN: Nonsense! Shut your eyes and keep repeating it.

HONEY-OF-LIFE *appears, looking round entrance.*

HONEY (*to* VIZIER): Vizzie-Wizzie! (*Embraces* VIZIER)

VIZIER (*embarrassed*): Ahem! (*Indicates presence of* SULTAN)

HONEY (*entering and prostrating herself*): O Commander of the Faithful! I did not recognize you, with your back turned and without your crown.

SULTAN (*turning to her*): Eh? Get up, girl! (*Raising her*) Dear me—a very pretty face. You are to treat me exactly as you would treat the Vizier.

HONEY: Exactly as I would treat the Vizier? (*Astonished*)

SULTAN: Yes. He says the idea is painful to him.

HONEY: I dare say. He is frightfully jealous.

SULTAN: I don't see what jealousy has to do with it. All I want you to do is to treat me exactly as you would him; that will give him a lesson.

HONEY: Do you really mean it, O King?

SULTAN: Don't call me "O King." Address me as you would him.

HONEY: Well—if I must, I must. Sit down, Vizzie-Wizzie!

SULTAN (*sitting on step of throne*): Eh?

HONEY (*sitting beside him*): There! (*Kisses him*)

SULTAN: Dear me! And what would the Vizier do?

VIZIER (*angrily*): He would say, "Keep your place, naughty girl—and I will keep mine."

SULTAN: A good idea. (*to* HONEY-OF-LIFE) Keep your place, naughty girl—and er—yes—I will keep mine. Would the Vizier do this? (*Kisses her*)

VIZIER: Certainly not!

SULTAN: Then he can have no objection to my doing it.

Kisses her as enter DANCING SUNBEAM *and* BLUSH-OF-MORNING (*followed by* HEART'S DESIRE)

(NOTE: *The libretto has "Song-of-Nightingales" entering at this point, not "Heart's Desire." The vocal score has Heart's Desire taking the mezzo-soprano (third) line of the next song, and so I have indicated the character here and omitted Song-of-Nightingales.—ed.*)

SUNBEAM: That is exactly what I expected.
SULTAN: Indeed, madam? Well—the other Vizier is disengaged.
  (*Kisses* HONEY-OF-LIFE)
SUNBEAM: You will both be disengaged very quickly, if you don't do as I bid you. Lead me to the Sultana's apartments.
SULTAN: Who is this?
HONEY: Oh, I came to announce them. They are a Deputation.
BLUSH: We are wives of the man called Hassan, who, we learned last night, is no other than the Sultan.
SUNBEAM: And I claim my rights.
SULTAN: Do you mean that you wish to be recognized as the Sultana?
SUNBEAM: Precisely. I am the Sultana!
VIZIER: She undoubtedly is—if Hassan is Sultan. What will Rose-in-Bloom say, eh? (*Digs* SULTAN *in ribs*—SULTAN *rather annoyed*)
SULTAN: And you consider yourself fitted to take exalted rank?
SUNBEAM: Emphatically!

SONG.—DANCING SUNBEAM, with BLUSH-OF-MORNING, HONEY-OF-LIFE, HEART'S DESIRE, SULTAN, VIZIER, and PHYSICIAN.

SUNBEAM: In the heart of my hearts I've always known—
OTHERS: She's always known—
SUNBEAM: I've always known
  I should one day grace a social throne!
OTHERS: A social throne she'd grace!
SUNBEAM: I dreamed at the age of slim fifteen—
OTHERS: Far dim fifteen—
SUNBEAM: Of slim fifteen
  I should be what you see—a Social Queen!
OTHERS: Then take your proper place!
SUNBEAM: For to stand at the top
    Of a wide staircase,
  Till you're fit to drop
    With a fixed grimace
OTHERS: (*That is meant for a smile
    Of enjoyment keen*),
      Is the way
      To be gay

    As a Social Queen—
  And that's your proper, proper place!
ALL: That's your proper, proper place!
SUNBEAM: There are women I've known, and I sha'n't forget—
OTHERS: She can't forget—
SUNBEAM: I sha'n't forget—
  Who were Queens in my suburban set—
OTHERS: A far inferior race!
SUNBEAM: They'll learn there's a wider gap between—
OTHERS: A gap between—
SUNBEAM: A gulf between
  Them and me (*you'll see*) now I'm a Queen!
OTHERS: You'll put them in their place!
SUNBEAM: For to turn up your nose
     At the people who
  Are precisely those
     Who have once snubbed you—
OTHERS: For to patronize them,
     Or to cut them clean,
        Is the height
        Of delight
     To a Social Queen!
  And that's your proper, proper place!
ALL: That's your proper, proper place!

DANCE.

Exeunt DANCING SUNBEAM, HONEY-OF-LIFE, BLUSH-OF-MORNING, (HEART'S DESIRE,) *and* PHYSICIAN.

SULTAN (*to* VIZIER): Where have they gone?

VIZIER: Honey-of-Life is taking them to the western door of the Harem.

SULTAN: But before they go in there, my joke must be explained to Rose-in-Bloom. She won't understand another lady marching in, calling herself Sultana. Run after Honey-of-Life!

VIZIER: I had been running after her for weeks, when you just now took up the running.

SULTAN: Tut, tut, man! That was part of the joke—one of the best parts. Go and tell Honey-of-Life to tell Rose-in-Bloom about Hassan.

VIZIER: I hear and obey. (*At exit*) Rose-in-Bloom shall be told the whole of your joke—especially the best part. (*Exit L.U.E.*)

SULTAN (*calling after him*): No—not that part!

Enter HEART'S DESIRE, *R.U.E.*

DESIRE: O King, the favoured Rose-in-Bloom approaches, praying for an audience.

SULTAN: Is she coming from the western door?

DESIRE: No, O King—from the eastern.

SULTAN: It is well. (*Going quickly to L.U.E., then turning*) Tell her, if you see her first, that another lady is calling herself Sultana—in a moment I will return and tell her why.

Exit SULTAN.

Enter SCENT-OF-LILIES.

DESIRE: A new Sultana!

SCENT: What's the matter?

Enter ROSE-IN-BLOOM.

DESIRE: The Sultan has disgraced Rose-in-Bloom. Another Sultana is already installed in her place.

ROSE: What?

SCENT: Ah!

DESIRE: He has ordered me to tell you.

SCENT: What did I tell you?

DESIRE: In a moment he will return and tell you why.

ROSE: There's no need for that. He has found out everything.

Enter SULTAN.

SULTAN: Ah! Here you are! You heard my message?

ROSE: Yes. Pardon!

DESIRE: Pardon!

SCENT: I know it's very little use, but—pardon!

SULTAN: I beg your pardon—what do you mean?

Enter HONEY-OF-LIFE.

ROSE, SCENT, and DESIRE: We didn't mean any harm—we didn't mean anything wrong. Pardon!

HONEY: Pardon!

SULTAN (*to* HONEY): What do you want?

HONEY: The Vizier sent me to help you explain your joke to the Sultana. He says he is sure you will forget the best part.

SULTAN: Ah! I prefer to talk to the Sultana privately.

Rose, Scent, and Desire: To the Sultana? (*Looking at one another*) Is she/Am I still the Sultana?

Sultan: Now I think I understand. Dear me! You misunderstood my message. I am obliged to allow a certain lady to call herself Sultana as part of a joke I am playing on a man named Hassan.

Rose: A joke?

Sultan: Yes.

Honey: The Vizier told me to remind you that you said the best part of the joke—

Sultan: Yes, I remember. (*To* Rose-in-Bloom) Would you mind dismissing these girls?

Rose: Oh, I don't mind anything now!

Sultan: You really thought you were disgraced! And it was only part of a joke. Ha! Ha! Ha!

Girls (*forcing a laugh*): Ha! Ha! Ha!

Sultan: But what did you imagine you had been disgraced for?

Rose: Oh, well—(*to* Girls) Why, I didn't really think I had been. Did I?

Sultan: But you were praying for pardon—what for?

Desire: Oh, that was part of our joke! Ha! Ha! Ha! (*forced laugh*)

Girls: Yes, that was our joke! Ha! Ha!

Exeunt Heart's Desire *and* Scent-of-Lilies, *with forced laugh.*

Honey: The Vizier says he won't speak to me again if I forget to remind you that you said the best part of your joke was—

Sultan: Yes—I remember—run away!

Exit Honey-of-Life.

Rose: Haven't you told me all of the joke?

Sultan: My dear, the whole matter is that I went last night in disguise to the house of a man named Hassan—

Rose: Yes, I know.

Sultan: Do you? How?

Rose: Well, I declare—I must have dreamed that you did! I often dream of you going about in disguise—and—and meeting other girls—and—and kissing them.

Sultan: Dreams generally have nothing to do with what has really occurred.

Rose: No—that's what comforts me. Now the other night I had an absurd dream that I actually went out of the Palace in disguise.

Sultan: How ridiculous!

Rose: Wasn't it? Suppose I ever did such a thing—what would the punishment be?

Sultan: Oh, death, I suppose.

Rose: Are you sure?

Sultan: I might try to think of something worse. It would depend, of course, on my mood. Why do you want to know?

Rose: Because, in my dream, you did find me out, and said, "Oh, well, you've done no real harm—I sha'n't punish you at all."

Sultan: How absurdly people talk in their dreams, don't they?

Duet.—Rose-in-Bloom and Sultan.

Rose: Suppose—I say suppose—
   That your silly ickle wife
   Just for once in all her life
   Were to foolishly forget
   Oriental etiquette
   And infringe a regulation
   Formed for persons of her station—
   Would oo blame oo ickle wifie?
   Would oo punish wifie-pifie?
   (*Earnestly* Would she meet a dreadful doom?

Sultan: Suppose my lovely Rose,
     My Royal Rose-in-Bloom,
   My Royal spouse Zubeydeh,
   Could forget she is a lady—
   Then my silly ickle wifie
   Oo would lose oo ickle lifie!

Ensemble.

Sultan.	Rose-in-Bloom.
For queens must not forget, My pet,	For queens must not forget Their "set,"
They owe to etiquette A debt;	They owe to etiquette A debt;
And Royalty must ever be Upheld in perfect dignity!	And Royalty must ever be Upheld in perfect dignity!

Rose: Suppose—I say suppose—
　　That one night she couldn't sleep,
　　So she thought that she would creep
　　Like a silent little mouse
　　Down the stairs and out the house
　　And about the city trotted—
　　Would she have to be garotted?
　　Would a nasty knifie-pifie
　　Put an end to ickle wifie
　　　　Or a bow-string be her doom?
Sultan: My wifie-pifie knows,
　　　　My Royal Rose-in-Bloom,
　　If she did what you refer to,
　　Then the Executioner to,
　　With his great big knifie-pifie,
　　I should send my ickle wifie!

Ensemble.

Sultan.	Rose-in-Bloom.
But as I can't suppose	But as you can't suppose
My Rose	Your Rose,
Forgetting what she knows	Forgetting what she knows
She owes	She owes
To rigid Royal etiquette,	To rigid Royal etiquette,
We will not talk of that, my pet!	We will not talk of that, as yet!

Chorus *enter with* Hassan, *who is carried in still unconscious, and set upon the throne. He is dressed in Royal garments.*

Scene.

Chorus: Laughing low,
　　　On toe-tip,
　　Finger so—
　　　On each lip!
　　Whispering,
　　　(*Undertone,*)
　　Set the King
　　　On the throne!

>   King Hassan!
>   Ho! ho! ho! ho! ho! ho!
>   Laugh pian—
>   Issimo. Ho! ho! ho!
>   Hush, hush, hush, hush!
> *They watch* HASSAN, *who slowly begins to wake.*
> HASSAN (*opening his eyes*):
>   Where am I—where?
> VIZIER: Where art thou—where
>   But in thy palace rich and rare,
>   Where none can say thee nay.
> CHORUS: Where everyone
>   Will rush and run
>   And race to get thy bidding done—
>   We hear thee and obey!
> HASSAN (*astonished*): But hear me speak—
> PHYSICIAN: But hear him speak,
>   And other music's flat and weak
>   Beside his golden speech!
> CHORUS: His lightest word
>   Is far preferred
>   Beyond the music any bird
>   Could ever hope to reach!
> HASSAN (*more bewildered*):
>   Attend to me—
> EXECUTIONER: Attend to him
>   And bring a goblet to the brim
>   With Persian sherbet filled!
> CHORUS: And when he dips
>   His Royal lips
>   Let dainty damask catch the drips,
>   That none of them be spilled!
>   Attend to him!
> HASSAN: Has Dancing Sunbeam had the house re-decorated, and invited a party while I've been asleep? (*To* VIZIER) Is this my house?
> VIZIER: O King, are you not the Sultan?
> HASSAN: Don't be silly! If this is a joke on the part of my wives, it is a very cheap form of wit—or very expensive. These decorations—

(*looking round, he sees the* EXECUTIONER) Aren't you the Sultan's Executioner?

EXEC.: Yes—I am your Executioner.

HASSAN: My Executioner! (*In a sudden access of terror*) I remember now. I'm going to be executed. Mercy! Mercy! (*Throws himself at feet of the* EXECUTIONER)

Enter SULTAN.

SULTAN: What is happening to the Commander of the Faithful?

PHYS.: I think that while he slept he was troubled by a bad dream, and the shadow of his nightmare still lingers with him.

SULTAN: Is that so, O King?

HASSAN (*after a pause*): A dream! Would it be possible that everything that is real I should have forgotten, and that everything I remember is only a dream?

PHYS.: Quite.

HASSAN: And who are you?

PHYS.: Your Physician-in-Chief, O King. Do you not know me?

HASSAN: No. And yet I seem to have a cloudy recollection of having seen you somewhere—and you—and you (*to* VIZIER, SULTAN, *and* EXECUTIONER) (*To* EXECUTIONER) I actually recognised you, didn't I?

EXEC.: O King, it was a great joy to me.

HASSAN: Somehow it wasn't to me. Do you really mean to say that I am the Sultan?

SULTAN: May your shadow never grow less.

HASSAN: Talking of growing less—how is it that my clothes fit so badly? I seem to have shrunk.

SULTAN: O King, you have just awakened from a long illness.

HASSAN: Have I?

SULTAN: That is why your memory and your body have both shrunk.

HASSAN: My memory has simply shrunk to nothing. Except my delirium, I can't remember—Have you ever heard of a man called Hassan—whom folks call "Mad Hassan"?

VIZIER: Mad Hassan?

SULTAN: Who is he, O King?

HASSAN: I—I don't quite know.

SULTAN: Is there such a man, O King?

HASSAN: I—I'm not quite sure. (*Almost weeps. Buries his face in his hands*)

VIZIER (*to* SULTAN): Shall the people enter who crave audience?
SULTAN: Yes. You have warned them they are to address him as if he were myself?
VIZIER: Yes, O King.
SULTAN: Anything he grants wisely I will confirm.
VIZIER (*reading from list*): Yussuf, a Story-Teller, craves a boon of the Full Moon of Full Moons.
Enter HEART'S DESIRE.
SULTAN: Bring Yussuf, the Story-Teller! (*Enter* HONEY-OF-LIFE)
VIZIER: Yussuf, the Story-Teller! (*Enter* SCENT-OF-LILIES)
PHYS.: Yussuf, the Story-Teller!
EXEC.: Yussuf, the Story-Teller! (*Enter* YUSSUF)
YUSSUF: I am here—Yussuf, the Story-Teller!
DESIRE (*aside to* YUSSUF): Be very careful!
SCENT (*aside*): Mind what you say!
HONEY (*aside*): Don't get flustered!
YUSSUF: I have come to—to—that is to say—
HASSAN *has raised his head and is regarding him earnestly.*
SULTAN: To say what?
YUSSUF: That I would ask for one of the Royal Slaves for a wife!
HASSAN: Listen: did you meet the slave at the house of a man named Hassan?
YUSSUF: No—er—O King!
HASSAN: Do you know a man named Mad Hassan?
YUSSUF: No—er—O King!
HASSAN: It is most extraordinary. (*Sinks back. Then leans forward and points to* HEART'S DESIRE) Is not that the slave you would take to wife?
YUSSUF: No—I don't know her—I don't know Hassan—I don't know—
SULTAN: Don't you know whom you do want to marry?
YUSSUF: No.
HASSAN: Young man, you seem to be one of those who rush very blindly into matrimony. Remember, that in the matter of wives you will find that five-and-twenty are practically—(*To* SULTAN) How many wives have I?
SULTAN: In the Royal Harem there are six hundred and seventy-one, O King.
HASSAN: Good gracious! You don't say so!

SULTAN: Stand back, O Story-Teller, and if your other stories equal this story of your love, I should join another profession.

DESIRE: I think you tell stories magnificently.

VIZIER: Abdallah the Priest begs an audience.

HASSAN: Eh?

SULTAN: Bring Abdallah the Priest.

DESIRE (*to* YUSSUF): If he speaks of the Sultana, you shall hear me tell my story. (*Goes up*)

VIZIER: Abdallah the Priest!

PHYS.: Abdallah the Priest!

EXEC.: Abdallah the Priest!

Enter ABDALLAH.

ABDALLAH: I am here—Abdallah the Priest!

HASSAN: Ah! Do you know a man that folks call Mad Hassan?

ABDALLAH: Yes, O King!

HASSAN: Where is he?

ABDALLAH: He is at the point of death.

HASSAN: Why—why do you think that?

ABDALLAH: Because, when the Sultan knows that his Sultana visited this man's house last night, he will assuredly put Hassan to death.

SULTAN: Is this true, Hassan?

HASSAN: Then I am Hassan!

SULTAN: And I am the Sultan!

HASSAN: Well, I'm not sorry! Six hundred and seventy-one wives—and I've not forgotten my past life!

SULTAN: Make the most of the recollection—for you have little enough in the future, if this be true. Speak, dog!

ABDALLAH: It is true, O King. I saw the Sultana in his house, wearing the Royal signet.

HASSAN: O King, it is true that she dropped in—unexpectedly—but if you will listen to me—

SULTAN: Listen, dog! Have I not heard enough? (*To* EXECUTIONER, *who has moved across*) Slay this man! And the Sultana—Rose-in-Bloom—she favours low company; marry her to the Story-Teller, who wants a wife, and cares not who it is. I have spoken.

DESIRE: O King—hear me! Rose-in-Bloom is innocent. The signet was worn by—

SULTAN: I have spoken.

Exeunt SULTAN *and* ABDALLAH.
SCENT: I said that idea wouldn't come off.

>QUINTET and CHORUS.—SCENT-OF-LILIES, HEART'S DESIRE, YUSSUF, HASSAN, and EXECUTIONER.

SCENT (*to* EXECUTIONER):
   It's a busy, busy, busy, busy day for thee
   Very busy, busy, busy must a morning be
      For any man
      Who has to plan
    For a wedding and a beheading.
EXECUTIONER: For the marriage order carriages at half-past two:
   (*to* HASSAN) And the block at two o'clock, but that will be for you!
      And, bless my heart,
      It's time to start,
    Or I shall be late for the wedding!
CHORUS: But bless my heart, etc.
YUSSUF (*to* DESIRE): Of overpowering high degree
   Th'exalted dame who marries me!
      But we must part,
      My own sweetheart,
      Must part, my true sweetheart!
SCENT (*to* DESIRE):
   It's a mise-mise-miserable day for thee!
   Ah! mise-miserable will the marriage be!
DESIRE (*to* YUSSUF): I'll plot and plan,
     And, if I can,
  Upset the fate you're dreading!
HASSAN (*to* YUSSUF):
   At your marriage, though the carriages
       obstruct the view,
   It's the block at two o'clock that
      I shall not get through!
     And bless my heart,
      It's time to start,
    Or I shall be late for beheading!
CHORUS: Or I shall be late for the wedding.

Ensemble.

Scent-of-Lilies, Yussuf.	Of overpowering high degree, etc.
Heart's Desire.	I'll plot and plan, etc.
Hassan, Executioner, Chorus.	It's a busy, busy, busy, busy day, etc.

Exeunt all except Yussuf *and* Heart's Desire.

Desire: So, if all goes ill, are you to marry Rose-in-Bloom instead of me?

Yussuf: Yes. Life seemed a poem; but as we read it by the light of Hope, Fate crept behind us and blew out the lantern.

Desire (*sighs*): Rose-in-Bloom is very beautiful.

Yussuf: What value has beauty to me when the whole world is pitch-dark?

Desire: If she were not young and beautiful—if she were middle-aged and quite plain—would you be just as pleased?

Yussuf: Just as displeased.

Desire: Are you sure? Absolutely certain?

Yussuf: Yes. It makes no difference to me.

Desire: It would to me. It's beastly of me, I know—but it would! But she is young and beautiful, and some day she will light the lantern again, and you will go on reading your poem, or another one that you think much nicer.

Yussuf: I think there is only one page of poetry in all the book of a man's life.

Desire: Only one page, perhaps. But it may have a lot of poems on it—little ones—all different. Your poetry page is likely to be immense.

Yussuf: Whatever it is, Fate is turning it over. The story is finished—the Bazaar is empty—the lights put out—and you and I must go out into the darkness.

Desire: But not hand-in-hand.

Song.—Yussuf.

Our tale is told,
And now is growing old!
   For Fate, who holds the book
     Of childhood, youth, and age,
  Her finger now doth crook

>   To turn another page.
> Try to forget—
> Although a soft regret
>   Like some poor faded rose-leaf life
>   (*To mark the place*)
>   Within the book where thou and I
>   Have read one passage full of grace!
> Try to forget!
> The desert's wide—
> And we must mount and ride!
>   Each with a caravan
>   That's laden with our sighs;
>   To barter, if we can,
>   Our loads in Paradise.
> Try to forget!
> Our caravans have met
>   Amid the burning desert space,
>   Where thou and I
>   Have rested in a shady place
>   A little while, and then passed by!
> Try to forget!

Exit Yussuf, *leaving* Heart's Desire. *Enter* Rose-in-Bloom.

Rose: Heart's Desire, I have been summoned to the ceremony of my divorce and disgrace! How am I looking?

Desire: Are you ready for your wedding with my Story-Teller?

Rose: Cannot you do anything to save me?

Desire: I wish I could. I tried to tell the Sultan that it was only myself impersonating you at Hassan's house, but he wouldn't listen.

Enter Blush-of-Morning.

Rose: He might later on—if we could only put it off.

Enter Scent-of-Lilies, *then* Honey-of-Life.

Blush: Oh, which one of you is the Sultana?

Rose: I am—for a minute or two longer.

Blush: Well, Dancing Sunbeam says you left off being Sultana half an hour ago, when she came. And she wants to know if it is true that a message has just been sent to the Sultana, and, if so, why it was not brought to her!

Honey: The Sultan did say she was to be treated as Sultana.

Scent: Do you thing we could manage?—

DESIRE: Yes. Yussuf said he wouldn't mind if she were middle-aged and plain, and I'm bound to believe him; and it would comfort me.

SCENT: Here she comes! (*Drums*)

HONEY: And here's the Executioner!

DESIRE (*to* ROSE): Run back—to the eastern door. She shall take your place.

Exit ROSE-IN-BLOOM. *Enter* DANCING SUNBEAM.

SUNBEAM: Are you not aware that I am Sultana—and that it was I who should have been summoned to this ceremony, whatever it is?

BLUSH: They understand now. They made a mistake.

SCENT, HONEY, *and* DESIRE. *We apologize.*

SUNBEAM: Well, well, you can enlighten me on a small point of etiquette that, curiously enough, I am ignorant of. Should I be veiled, or not, for this ceremony?

SCENT: Of course.

DESIRE: It is most important!

HONEY: There will be men present—horrid men! Don't you know that the Queen's face must never be seen by any man but the Sultan? (*They begin arranging the veil*)

SUNBEAM: Men are absurdly jealous!

BLUSH: But what is the ceremony?

SUNBEAM: I have an idea that I am to be publicly acknowledged Queen. In a few minutes you will see me attain the summit of even my Ararat of ambition!

She is veiled—the GIRLS *twist her round, humming:*

GIRLS: Giddy girl this way, giddy girl that,
Say if the world be round or flat!
Say if the world be upside down!
Which will you marry, a King or a Clown?

Exeunt HONEY-OF-LIFE *and* HEART'S DESIRE. *Enter* EXECUTIONER (*followed by a* ROYAL GUARD).

EXEC.: Is the Sultana here?

SUNBEAM: I am she.

SCENT (*going to him*): Yes, that is she!

EXEC.: When I have pronounced the decree your veil will be removed, that all and sundry, high and low, may gaze upon your beauty.

SUNBEAM: A very good idea.

SCENT (*to* EXECUTIONER): You have never seen the Sultana's face, have you?

Exec.: No man has, except the Sultan. You ought to know that.

Scent: The reason I mention it is, if you had, you will find her greatly changed. The anxiety she has gone through during the last half-hour has added at least twenty-five years to her appearance; even her voice has turned into a contralto. (*Exit*)

Exec.: Bring in the Story-Teller. (*Enter* Yussuf) I am going to pronounce the decree.

Sunbeam: Don't waste any more time. (*The* Executioner *unfolds a scroll*)

Exec.: By the decree of the Sultan, I pronounce you divorced—eternally disgraced—and married to this vagabond. Remove your veil—take twopence from the poor-box—go in peace—I have spoken.

The veil is removed—Picture.

Sunbeam: What did you say?   }
Blush: What did it mean?   }   (*together*)
Yussuf: Married to her?   }

Exec.: The thing's quite plain.

Yussuf: It is. And middle-aged. This is what Heart's Desire meant.

Exec.: You're married. It's all over. Now it's over, I don't mind acknowledging I'm sorry for both of you. I've never felt any qualms at executing anybody; but marrying 'em is different. I'm not a marrying man. Scent-of-Lilies says I am—but I'm not. It upsets me. (*Exit*)

Recitative and Quartet.—Blush-of-Morning, Dancing Sunbeam, Yussuf, and a Royal Guard.

Blush-of-Morning, Dancing Sunbeam, and Yussuf.

What does it mean?
Yussuf: Upon what hidden trap
   Have I now stumbled?
Sunbeam: One moment Queen
   Then comes a thunderclap
Trio: And I lie humbled!
Yussuf: So surely swings the pendulum of Fate
   That maketh joy and sorrow alternate.
Quartet: Joy and sorrow alternate:
   Every hour that passeth by

Till tomorrow fickle Fate
    May ordain you laugh or cry!
So the clock that strikes the time
Rings at first a merry chime;
Then, to mock the marriage bell,
Tolls a melancholy knell!
Or the melancholy gong
Tolls a solitary "Dong!"
A Dong! Dong! Dong!
Then you hear the joy-bells ring,
Ring-a-ding-a-dong-a-dong!
So the clock doth indicate
Joy and sorrow alternate!
    Ding! dong! Ding! dong!

Exeunt YUSSUF, SOLDIER, *and* BLUSH-OF-MORNING. *Enter* SCENT-OF-LILIES, *followed by* HEART'S DESIRE, *followed by* VIZIER—*all excitedly.*

SCENT: Stop the marriage!

DESIRE: Don't go on with it!

VIZIER: Delay the wedding!

THREE (*together*): Where's the Executioner?

Enter EXECUTIONER.

EXEC.: Here! (*He brings on* HASSAN) The wedding is over.

VIZIER: Over! But the Sultan has relented!

SCENT: And is going to give the Sultana the chance of an explanation.
    (SUNBEAM *looks up*)

Enter PHYSICIAN *and* SULTAN.

PHYS.: O King, you are too late!

SULTAN (*to* EXECUTIONER): Dog, what have you done?

SUNBEAM (*to* HASSAN): An explanation! It's high time I had an explanation from you! How dare you let this brute divorce me and marry me to a wretched Story-Teller?

HASSAN (*to* EXECUTIONER): Have you divorced her and married her to someone else?

EXEC.: Yes. It went against the grain—I'm not a marrying man!

HASSAN (*taking his hand*): I don't know why you have done it, but let me thank you for lightening the gloom of my declining moments.

SULTAN: Is it you who have been married?

SUNBEAM: Who else? Have you had a hand in it?

SULTAN: My dear Executioner, you've made a mistake.
EXEC.: Yes, O King! I've always looked on marriage as unlucky.
SCENT: Nonsense!
EXEC.: Shall I execute myself at once—or wait till I've finished this?
HASSAN: Don't wait for me.
SULTAN: You've married the wrong woman! That's all. I'm very pleased. I'll see about restoring this lady to her proper husband when I have time.
HASSAN: Not during the next five minutes. I am to be beheaded in five minutes. Wait till after that!
SULTAN: Very well!
SUNBEAM (*to* HASSAN): Do you mean to say you're not the Sultan?
HASSAN: Go and talk to your husband.
Exit SUNBEAM. *Enter* ABDALLAH.
DESIRE: O King, hear me now. It was I who was at this man's house. It was I who wore the Sultana's Royal Ring, and showed it to the Priest. It was I who called myself Sultana. Ask him.
SULTAN: Is this so?
ABDALLAH: It was even so. Is not this Rose-in-Bloom? (*Indicates* HEART'S DESIRE)
SULTAN: Then Rose-in-Bloom is innocent—and has been falsely accused! (*To* ABDALLAH) You shall die!
HASSAN: Another three minutes and it would have been too late for me, O King. I suppose you will have to go through the form of granting me the usual free pardon for what I never did!
SULTAN: Pardon you! No, indeed! You distinctly said my Royal Rose-in-Bloom did visit you, Dog! and so besmirched her Royal character with calumny. You shall die! And this slave who brought the name of Rose-in-Bloom into such contempt, she shall die! You shall all die—you and the Priest and the slave! I have spoken.
Enter HONEY-OF-LIFE.
HONEY: The Royal Rose-in-Bloom approaches!
VIZIER: Let all men turn away their faces. (*Men turn their backs. Enter* ROSE-IN-BLOOM)
ROSE: Let my slave live, O husband! Just to please me!
SULTAN: Have you any reason why this girl should not be executed?
ROSE: Yes, indeed! She—the fact is—she—(*to* HEART'S DESIRE)—say something!

Desire: O King, the Sultana is much given to letting me tell stories for her amusement. She is much interested in a story I am engaged in telling her now.

Rose: Yes, that's it! She has been telling such a lovely story for me—and I do want to know that it ends happily!

Sultan: Very well. She shall live until she has finished her story. Is it a very interesting story, and original?

Desire: Yes, O King.

Sultan: Where did you get it from?

Hassan: From me, that's why she has been in the habit of visiting me. I am telling it to her in instalments. I merely mention this because if I am executed I sha'n't be able to finish it to her, and she won't be able to finish it to the Sultana. That's all. It's quite immaterial to me.

Sultan: You shall be spared till the story is finished. Is it funny?

Hassan: Excruciating!

Sultan: And has a happy ending?

Hassan: A happy ending! It has a dozen!

Sultan: I will return in three minutes and listen to it myself. Come, Rose-in-Bloom. (*To* Hassan) You are sure it has a happy finish? I abominate unhappy endings.

Exeunt all except Hassan, Abdallah, Honey-of-Life, *and* Heart's Desire.

Hassan: So do I. But I don't think I am going to have one after all.

Desire: Why, all we have to do is think of a story that's so interesting and funny and long, that we can go on telling it for years and years without boring the Sultan, and we shall be all right.

Honey: Yes, that's all you have to think of—in three minutes.

Hassan: Two and a half now!

Abdallah: Tell the Sultan you get your story in instalments from me—and I will help you—think of one.

Hassan: And give me back my will?

Abdallah: Yes. (*Hands document, which* Hassan *tears up*)

Hassan: Very well. Now out with your story!

Abdallah: I haven't thought of one yet.

Hassan: I've got as far as that! (*Enter* Executioner *and* Scent-of-Lilies) Do you know any good stories?

Exec.: What?

Hassan: Can you tell me anything interesting, but funny, that has ever happened to you, that it would take a long time to repeat?

EXEC.: The funniest thing that has ever happened to me has happened just now. Scent-of-Lilies has persuaded me to propose to her, and I've been accepted!
HASSAN: And now I suppose you can think of nothing else?
EXEC.: Nothing else. I'm dazed! (*Exit*)
SCENT: He is so happy. (*Following him*)
HASSAN (*detaining her*): Then let him alone and stay here and help me think of a funny story—that will do for the Sultan.
Enter YUSSUF, *followed by* DANCING SUNBEAM.
HASSAN (*to* YUSSUF): The very man! I want a very long, interesting, funny story at once—to save my life with. Can you help me?
YUSSUF: No: I can think of nothing now but my marriage with your wife.
HASSAN: How abominably selfish young newly-married couples are!
SUNBEAM: I will help you. The Sultan said he would rectify this absurd marriage. And if he does, I shall want to come back to you.
HASSAN: Do you know, I'm not so sure it's worth while to bother about a story at all. I really begin to think it's better to let the law take it's course.
SUNBEAM: Think of me, dear!
HASSAN: I am!
DESIRE (*jumping up*): Oh, I've just thought—no, that won't do for the Sultan!
HASSAN: Once upon a time—no, that won't do for the Sultan!
SUNBEAM: Listen! Do you think this will do—I'm sure no one has heard it before.
HASSAN: I suppose it's only some silly bit of scandal—or we shouldn't hear it now.
SEPTET.—SCENT-OF-LILIES, HONEY-OF-LIFE, HEART'S DESIRE, DANCING SUNBEAM, YUSSUF, HASSAN, *and* ABDALLAH.
SUNBEAM: It has reached me a Lady named Hubbard
Proceeded one day to her cupboard,
    And openly went
    With intent to present
Her poor dog with a bone from her cupboard.
SCENT: And the dog of that person named Hubbard
Accompanied her to the cupboard;
    But when they got there
    They were plunged in despair—

There was nothing at all in the cupboard!
ALL: There was nothing whatever at all in the cupboard!
SCENT: Have you heard of that harrowing story?
HONEY: I have—it's in my category!
YUSSUF: And I!
DESIRE: So have I!
ABDALLAH: So have I!
HASSAN: So have I!
ALL: It's a horribly harrowing story!
    So that won't do for the Sultan
        To make him rejoice and exult! An
            Unfortunate end
            Will his temper offend
    So that won't do for the Sultan!
DESIRE: It is said a young lady named Muffet
    (*Selecting a seat on a tuffet*)
        Was breaking her fast
        With a modest repast
    When she suddenly fled from the tuffet!
HONEY: She spied a she-spider beside her!
    The spider beside her espied her!
        Beside herself she
        Would undoubtedly be
    Having spied a big spider beside her!
ALL: Having spied a big spider beside her!
SUNBEAM: Have you heard of that horrible story?
DESIRE: I have—it's in my category!
YUSSUF: And I!
SCENT: So have I!
ABDALLAH: So have I!
HASSAN: So have I!
ALL: It's a horribly harrowing story!
    So that won't do for the Sultan, etc.
YUSSUF: Have you heard of the "Hey-diddle-diddle,"
    That quaint zoological riddle,
        The cat they accuse
        Of invoking her "mews"
    On a stringed instrument called a fiddle?
HASSAN: At the cow, who was not an inert one,

The little dog laughed (*what a pert one!*);
> But oh, it is feared
> That the dish disappeared
With the tablespoon or the dessert one!

ALL: With the tablespoon or the dessert one!
SUNBEAM: Have you heard of that horrible story?
DESIRE: I have—it's in my category!
YUSSUF: And I!
SCENT: So have I!
ABDALLAH: So have I!
HASSAN: So have I!
ALL: It's a horribly harrowing story!
> So that won't do for the Sultan, etc.

As they are thinking of another tale, enter VIZIER, PHYSICIAN, *and* EXECUTIONER.

SCENE.

VIZIER: Hassan, the Sultan with his Court approaches!
> All looking forward to your story!

PHYSICIAN: I trust the Sultan won't be disappointed—
EXECUTIONER: For that means your execution!
Enter CHORUS.
CHORUS: Comes the King and all his Court
> Anxious to be testing
If your story be the sort
> Tale that's interesting.
If you've not yet got a plot
> He won't think you're jesting,
You will perish on the spot,
> Now isn't that interesting!

The SULTAN *enters.*
VIZIER: The royal Rose-in-Bloom unveiled approaches,
> Let all men turn respectful backs upon her!

ROSE-IN-BLOOM *enters and goes to* SULTAN.
SULTAN: Now, Hassan, we are ready for your story!
> Remember, though the plot may not allow it,
> I do command it have a happy ending—begin! begin!

HASSAN (*nervously*): Ahem!

SULTAN: Commence—I am impatient!
HASSAN (*nervously*): Ahem!
SULTAN: Go on!
BLUSH-OF-MORNING *whispers to* HASSAN.
HASSAN (*aside*): Ah! Happy thought! I'll try it!

SONG.—HASSAN.

There was once a small Street Arab,
    And perhaps his little name was Tom;
And he lived in Gutter-Persia
    Where street arabs rightly all come from;
And like little Gutter-Persians
    (*Every one and one and all*)
His young spirits were elastic
    As an India-rubber ball!
CHORUS: His young spirits were elastic as a ball!
HASSAN: And all day long he sang a song
    A merry little ditty as he danced a cellar-flap:
"The life I lead is all I need,
    I know no better"—the lucky little chap!
CHORUS: The life I lead, etc.
HASSAN: Now among the bricks and mortar
    Did his wretched little lifetime pass;
He had never seen a flower
    Or a single, simple blade of grass;
But one day he found a daisy,
    And he thought that simple thing
Was a wondrous flower from heaven,
    And he took it to the King.
CHORUS: And he took that simple daisy to the King.
HASSAN: He meant no wrong, and through the throng
    He struggled to the Sultan and then laid it on his lap;
(*That simple weed—he did indeed*),
    He knew no better—the stupid little chap!
CHORUS: That simple weed, etc.
HASSAN: But the Sultan gravely thanked him, saying
    "Would that would that I were wise
Enough to take a daisy

> For a lovely flower from Paradise!
> But I will not now reward thee,
> > Or exchange thy simple lot
> For great riches would but rob thee
> > Of a wealth that I have not!"

CHORUS: Would but rob thee of a wealth that I have not!
HASSAN: So all day long he sang his song
> A merry little ditty as he danced a cellar-flap:
"The life I lead is all I need!"
> He knew no better—the lucky little chap!

CHORUS: The life I lead, etc.
SULTAN: Is the story finished?
HASSAN: That is only the beginning, O King. That little boy was myself—and the Sultan was your father—and the story I have been telling to the slave, which she has been telling to the Sultana, is the story of my own life—and, O King, this is the point: you have yourself commanded that the story—which is my life—is to have a happy ending.
SULTAN: By the beard of my grandfather, you have played an odd trick upon me!
HASSAN: It is the odd trick, O King, that wins the game!
SULTAN: But not the rubber. Take back your wife—I restore her to you. (*Handing* SUNBEAM *to him*) I fancy that's the rub.
HASSAN: Yes, you've won. (YUSSUF *joins* HEART'S DESIRE)

FINALE OF ACT II.

ALL: A bridal march
> The funeral dirge becomes!
Let heaven's arch
> Re-echo the band of drum!
O happy pairs
> United this afternoon
We greet you one and all
Both great and small
> With popular Persian tune!
Oh, raise your voice
> In epithalamiums!
O King rejoice,

And Tale-Teller of the slums!
To high or low
    True love is an equal boon,
There's no one here too base
To find a place
    In popular Persian tune!
        Illalah! Illalah!

                End of Opera

Discover more of your favorite classics with Bookfinity™.

- Track your reading with custom book lists.
- Get great book recommendations for your personalized Reader Type.
- Add reviews for your favorite books.
- AND MUCH MORE!

Visit **bookfinity.com** and take the fun Reader Type quiz to get started.

Enjoy our classic and modern companion pairings!

Bookfinity is a registered trademark of Ingram Book Group LLC. © 2023 Bookfinity. All rights reserved.